BEYOND THE HORIZON

By
James C. Ellerbe

Not Enough Words LLC

Published by Not Enough Words LLC
www.JamesCEllerbe.com

The events and conversations in this book have been set down to the best of the author's ability, although some names and details have been changed to protect the privacy of individuals.

Second Edition: January 2019
First Edition: March 2015

Book cover by SpeechLOUD Enterprises
Photography by Stillmill Photography

ISBN: 978-1-7943-9977-8 (paperback)

Printed in the United States of America

Acknowledgements

First, all the honor and glory go to God for surrounding me with the right people and placing me in the right circumstances to change into the man He designed me to be. Second, I would like to thank my God-sent wife, Angela Ellerbe, for being the supportive wife that she always has been through this whole process, and for never letting me forget to put God first in anything I do. I love you so much; you are my inspiration and the reason why I work so hard to be the best husband I can be. You are my queen, my wife, and my everything. I would be remised to not thank my mother, Deborah Aultmon, the woman who taught me the ingredients that make a strong woman. This very lesson would later guide me to my wife. Thank you for giving birth to me and for raising me to be the man who can look you in the eye and know I made you proud. To Andre and Tyrell Aultmon, my brothers: You grew up with me and you put up with me, but you continue to love me.

I can't forget to name the people who influenced me along the way to chase this dream and to put my heart and soul into this craft. I will try to name them all, but, if I miss you, please forgive me. Know in your heart that you are a part of the development of this book. This is listed in no particular order, but I would like to thank: Wendi Dunlap, Jeff Carroll, Tina Thomas-

Perez, Alisha Williams, Prudence and Yamil Paez, Francesco Crocco, Ian Anderson, Takisha Carter-Homes, Fredrick Carter, Ronyel Clark, Aaron Jones, Tyrone Geralds, Chris "Flowmentalz" Cook, Helena D. Lewis, "Uninvited", Rob Hylton, Jamaal St. John, Jamal Hinnant, Shakira Malachi-Chang, Taalam Acey, Lamar Hill, Kamal Imani, "Backdraft", K. Desireé Milwood, and "Paradise." All of you played a huge part in the growth of my writing.

TABLE OF CONTENTS

FOREWORD

Rarely do we get to know what a poet is thinking, what shapes his words and deeds. A great poet is too often a mystery. The people wonder at the eloquence of the poet's words and draw inspiration from its profound effect; the scholars debate the poet's meaning throughout the ages and build careers on one interpretation or another. We may never know who or what was the inspiration behind William Shakespeare's dark lady or what is the meaning of John Keats' "La Belle Dame sans Merci." Not so with the Poet Ellerbe. In a rare and original volume, Ellerbe interweaves moments of lucid autobiographical prose with patches of poignant lyricism to tell the story of his life. In the process, he enlightens us to the pain and injustice that continue to ravage the lives of people of color in the United States; he also inspires us to overcome the many obstacles, both internal and external, that prevent us from pursuing our dreams.

Beyond the Event Horizon uses the motif of a black hole to convey the story of the poet's life. In Part 1: "Lost in Space," he describes the poet's painful adolescence growing up in the "hood" with an absent father and feeling like he does not belong. For a young black man, the gift of poetry can feel like a curse because it contradicts the norms of hyper-masculinity that too often characterize teen culture. Ellerbe waxes poetic on this subject in the volume's inaugural poem "The Outcast" in which he describes how he is harassed and misunderstood by his peers. The poet is figuratively lost in space as he struggles to find himself and understand his place in society. This journey takes the poet on an odyssey to find true love. It begins, as it always does, with painful disappointment. In "Love at First Sight," Ellerbe documents his fateful run-in with Asia and the blush of first love that follows. As the relationship degenerates, we feel the pain of love lost, first with tenderness in "The Dreamer," later with bitterness in "The Dreamer II (Time to Wake Up)." In "A Lost Sheep," Ellerbe invests his feelings of loss with a political edge by connecting them to the frustrations of a people lost and looking for leadership. This rich combination of the personal and the political will become a signature quality throughout the volume. "The Great O' US OF A." makes one of the strongest political statements in Part 1 by offering a powerful critique of racism, poverty, and injustice.

In Part 2: "Sucked in and Torn Apart," Ellerbe continues with the black hole motif to describe a dark period in his life. If Part 1 found him lost in space, Part 2 documents his untimely passage through the destructive vortex of a black hole. Black holes are impossibly dark because not even light can escape their gravitational pull. They are only visible by the perimeter of light and debris that encircles them. In scientific parlance, this perimeter is called the "event horizon" because it represents the point at which matter and energy are atomized and sucked into the void. In Ellerbe's life, the event horizon is his break-up with Asia, which sucks him into a vortex of nihilism and despair. In "The Player," he describes how the failure of love pulls him in the opposite direction; yet, in "Will You See Love" he continues to hope for a love that is real. Despite this personal setback, throughout this period we see the poet growing stronger in his trade and more confident in his calling. In "You Don't Love Me; You Love My Poetry," he embraces his emerging poetic self. In "Poems for P," he defends his profession against imposters who exploit the word for the flesh. With poems like "A Living Hell," he also hones his political critique into a fine edge by continuing to explore themes of racial and class injustice. The section ends with a plaintive lament, "I Got a Date with the Devil," in which he yearns for a better life.

Part 3: "Beyond the Event Horizon (Paradigm Shift)" is the culmination of the volume and the poet's life. Scientists theorize that black holes may be the umbilical cord to a new universe, and some believe that our own universe may have been created by a black hole. Matter is sucked in and ejected out the other side, providing substance for a new universe. Ellerbe uses this process of creative destruction to describe the arc of his own life. With the wisdom of hindsight, he realizes that he had to pass through the nihilism and despair of Part 2 in order to transform into a stronger, more confident, and more purposeful individual. Part 3 takes many of the themes of the previous parts—self-reflection, romantic longing, political awareness, and a desire for personal and political change—and restates them with greater assertiveness and maturity. In "Pain with No Chaser" and "A Better Man," the poet reflects on his pain and makes moves toward a better life. This section also offers some of the most original and thought-provoking political commentary in the volume with gems like "'Till Next We Meet at the Laundromat," "A Child That Doesn't Have Its Own," "Soul Survivor," "Blue," and The Great O' US OF A. II." Ellerbe also expands his social critique to cover the abuse of women in "The Evil That Men Do." Ellerbe's turn to Christianity is a major factor in his transformation, and "God-Mind" provides insight into his personal theology. Another factor in his transformation is his commitment to getting out of debt; two poems, "Money Matters" and "Mr. Poor" address this theme. Probably the most significant factor in Ellerbe's transformation is his reunion with love. "Define You," "The One," and the volume's concluding poem, "My Forever," complete the story of his odyssey for love by providing a happy ending with his marriage to Angela, his angel. Though not the final poem in the volume,

"Speak Life" offers perhaps the most poignant self-reflection on Ellerbe's incredible transformation from tortured adolescent to mature poet. With newfound confidence and resolve, it also challenges us to transform our lives and our world.

I would be remiss if I did not address the performative aspect of Ellerbe's poetry. Ellerbe, you see, is a successful spoken word artist whom many know by his stage name, "Akil the Poet." Each of the poems in this volume is meant to be heard, not just read, and many of them were written for the stage. I have witnessed firsthand the riveting effect of Akil's lyrical mastery. First, he draws us in with intimate details about his joys and sorrows; then he explodes our consciousness with penetrating social commentary. By marrying poetry with spoken word, Akil the Poet reaches back to the very beginning of poetry. The first poets—the ancient bards, scops, and minstrels—were all spoken word artists. They wrote lines meant to be sung for live audiences of kings and commoners alike. One day they rallied armies, the next they sang wedding songs or chanted funeral dirges. Akil the Poet continues in this great tradition by bringing poetry back to its roots in spoken word.

The stage name "Akil the Poet" has even greater significance, though. The name defiantly declares what the man so eloquently shows us in this volume. James

Ellerbe is above all a poet. Lost in space, torn apart by a black hole of personal crisis, what emerges beyond the event horizon is indisputably a poet. Welcome, brother. You have arrived.

Dr. Francesco Crocco

INTRODUCTION

If I had to identify the scariest object in the universe, it would have to be a black hole. Physicists theorize that the closer you come to one, the more inevitable your own destruction becomes. You can't fight it. You can't escape it. You're hopeless, in every aspect of the word. In my opinion, that's not even the scariest part. It's the mystery surrounding what happens after you pass through a black hole.

The event horizon is defined as, "the boundary around a black hole on and within which no matter or radiation can escape." [1] Scientists and mathematicians know what happens when matter reaches the event horizon, or "the point of no return," but what then? Where does everything go? Not to pretend I am Neil deGrasse Tyson, the famous African-American astrophysicist and cosmologist. The irony is that the only reason why we know black holes exist is due to their interactions with celestial bodies. I'm really channeling my inner nerd right now, but all credit has to go to my years of watching the History Channel and the Discovery Channel.

---

[1] "Event Horizon." Dictionary.com Unabridged. Random House, Inc. 17 Dec. 2014. <Dictionary.com http://dictionary.reference.com/browse/event horizon>.

But, I digress: It is our bewilderment – the not-knowing – which fuels our curiosity. Poetry, in this same fashion, stimulates our inquisitiveness and awe.

A lot of poems are pretty straight forward, but some poetry can be just as mysterious as knowing what happens beyond a black hole's "point of no return." Some poets work hard to create lines loaded with so many double entendre that they become confusing. This would cause any reader or listener to tune out even the most notable of poets. The hardest thing for a poet to do is to be creative enough to put together words and phrases that the audience can understand. In this process, we tend to lose people along the way. When this happens, we forfeit the opportunity to make that sublime connection which makes the reader or listener have a common mind. You would think this would be a poet's aim.

Remember that one poem you read in high school in which you had no clue what the author was talking about? The one that made the teacher give up any hope of having one of her class' bright minds decipher it? For me, that was the work of Edgar Allan Poe. I'm by no means trying to take away from the literary genius of Poe, but he happens to be one of the poets whose work I found hard to understand. This is because I would have to know the backdrop of the poems I was reading. If I knew the author's

2

background and thought process, along with the culture of the times, I could comprehend Mr. Poe.

But, what if you could know what happens beyond the event horizon of poetry? What if we are providing all of this context to make the poet more understandable, and possibly become more of a fan? And, wouldn't it be a plus if this information came from the poet directly?

Thus, the premise of this book of poetry is to present some poems with a narrative of the culture, style progression and thought process of yours truly. Not all of the poems have a narrative. Many are straightforward and can be interpreted as stated. The poems are organized under three themes: "Lost in Space," "Sucked in and Torn Apart" and "Beyond the Event Horizon (Paradigm Shift)." These themes provide the background, cultural context and thinking behind the creation of each particular piece.

This is a rare opportunity to really know what in the world was on my mind, or what influences conjured up the poems within me. The gloves are off. The poems are clearly told, but you are free to have your own interpretations. There's no more hiding behind words in hope that you won't see the silhouette of my psyche peering back at you. You know we poets love to do this to you sometimes, but not in this book. I am fully exposed by the words. Only the names have been changed to protect the innocent, me (sorry I had to).

This book is for all those who felt pain, love, sacrifice, happiness, and struggle. This book's sole purpose is to take you on a journey through my mind – to go *Beyond the Event Horizon* to better understand the man behind the pages.

Will you join me?

JOURNAL ENTRY — JANUARY 24, 1996

One of my biggest aspirations in life is to publish a book of poetry. A lot of people think I am obsessed with this poetry stuff, and say that I hide my true self in my work. Well, I do agree with them, since, for so long, I've been rejected by my peers. My poetry was another means of getting out what I felt, indirectly. Poetry became my outlet, my connection to myself and to the world. Now, I want to expose it.

This plan, which was manifested by letting one person read my poetry, has been the focus of my life. It has been brought to my attention that they have the ability to touch people. My poems have a way of letting people encounter what they feel in written form. This is my mission: to write this book.

CHAPTER 1: LOST IN SPACE

One of my favorite sci-fi movies of all time is "Alien." Even the tagline made you anxious: "In space, no one can hear you scream." Just thinking about the gravity of that scares me. Sound is pretty insignificant in the vastness of space. If you were in trouble or Lost in Space, no one would hear you. No distress signal to be heard; very parallel to my life.

If you would've asked me what my passion was when I was a freshman in high school, believe me when I say that I wouldn't have told you it was poetry. In the 90s, the natives of Hackensack, New Jersey's Railroad Avenue didn't give you cool points for writing verse, unless it was a "mean" 16-bar one. If you have no clue what I'm talking about, then your genre of music is obviously not hip-hop. My early days of writing poetry were masked underneath the rhymes I wrote to impress my peers.

Little did they know, I hid more pain into the pages of lyric-packed composition books than in a visit to a psychiatrist. Struggle bled onto those pages more profusely than in an Extreme Championship Wrestling barbed-wire match. There were plenty of so-called "love relationships" that ended in "love lost" to make the nicest guy want to give up on love forever.

The irony was I didn't consider those words to be poetry. In my mind, what I wrote was some sort of journal or diary. I was a teenager with no clue where I was going, got picked on by the neighborhood, and wasn't popular enough for the popular girls. There wasn't any anti-bullying campaign in those days. You had to pay your dues and cry your blues behind closed doors.

You can say I "danced with the Devil" many nights. I was one cry away from suicide and oblivion. I was the "oddball." People tolerated me because I was amusing to them at times. Shoot, even my own friends would call me "Forrest Gump." In those days, we had tough-love kind of friendships, or at least that's the kind of love I was getting. And, in those days, love was how many girls were "sweatin'" you.
Yep. There was solace in the pen.

There was solace, because no one, in those days, would listen to a young African-American boy with a mother one paycheck away from poverty (though she did the best she could as a single parent). No one would listen to a child whose father he barely saw. Half the time, we were - and, in some ways, still are - defending our image from the stereotypes of being "miscreant," "uneducated", "dysfunctional" and "lazy degenerates." Don't get me wrong, African-American girls have their share of troubles, and one doesn't supersede the other.

Plus, coming from a broken home (like many American families), I was forced to either resolve a lot of my problems on my own or through the misguidance of my fellow peers. It wasn't until later, in my junior and senior years of high school, that I felt comfortable enough to open up to my mother. Like most teenagers, I was living a double life: the good son that got good grades in school, and the "wannabe" stud who was failing miserably at dating. When I wasn't playing the role, the writing was my only escape. I later discovered that this was poetry.

The following pieces are from this point in my life. These words are pure in their honesty but are also a call for help like a child locked in a closet with no one around to get him out. I truly was Lost in Space. But, through it all, there was still a voice inside of me that refused to die, even though my spirit already seemed dead.

THE OUTCAST

I was that no-Adidas-wearing
No-Lee's-wearing brother in the past
Who sat in the front of the class
Because I always got harassed
From my "Japs"[2] to the clothes on my back,
From the things I liked
To the things I lacked.

I was that kid the girls never said "hi" to,
Always had to lie to
So my feelings wouldn't get hurt.
I was that no-name who never had the fame,
Never had any game.
I always rolled with the same people:
        Me,
        Myself
        And I,
But I was told that on the other side of the fence,
The grass is not greener.

I was that other guy
Who you passed on by,
Never offered a ride,
And laughed when I cried.

---

[2] It's not known where this slang term originated, but it was one used in my neighborhood for sneakers that were low budget, or off brand. Back in the early 90's kids would get ridiculed for wearing them.

I was that unnecessary extension
To whom you never paid attention
And whom you always had to mention
As the object of ridicule.

I didn't like school
Because I wasn't cool enough.
Life was always tough
For me to survive,
But I was told that on the other side of the fence,
The grass is not greener.

You were the one who was never-to-be-found,
Who never was around
And skipped town when I needed a helping hand.

You were my man,
But, when I got jumped, you ran.
You never gave a damn about me.
You never planned to be my true friend,
And, in the end,
Your true self had no place to hide.

You took my self-esteem,
But you can no longer take my pride
Because you are the one
Who's standing on the other side of the fence
Wanting something greener.

THE MAN FROM YESTERDAY

I'm not a man.
I'm just a shadow of a man
Who once was.
I am a silhouette of a man
Who once was.
I'm falling.
Who's going to catch me?
Someone's got to catch me
Before it's too late.
Where did I go wrong?
Where do I belong?
Where is the man from yesterday?
Have you seen him?
Where did he hide?
Does he feel what's inside of me?
It seems that no one can confide in me.
Somebody find the man from yesterday.
Let him know I need him
Before it's too late
So I do sit,
And, so, I do wait
For the man –
The man from yesterday.

ESCAPE FROM THE WORLD

Screams of Hell fill me as I leave this world.
Out of reality,
I begin my journey through the mental,
Experiencing thoughts of a diabolical nature,
A mentality that encompasses my state of existence,
A journey that takes me
Through analytical methods which baffles some,
Because they can't
Comprehend the complexity
Of my mind,
And that threatens others
Because my thoughts see
Right through them.

Escaping from the hells of the present world,
Only to enter
A three-dimensional universe
Filled with
        Light,
        Lust,
        Love,
        Darkness,
        And damnation.
The world around me seems stagnant
As I go further and further away from reality.

This is my world:

The world of derivatives,
    Revolution,
    And integrals.
The world of black queens,
Black dreams and black holes
Around my reflections.
This is my high.
This is my escape that makes me numb to reality.
My mind is the only solution
To this world of insanity –
My protection –
My escape from the world.

FEW MOMENTS

To Katie Lee Aultmon, my grandmother, one day I will see you again. *Written sometime after her funeral.*

I can't take back all those years
When you sat back in your chair,
And I only cared about
When could I play,
And didn't sit down to hear you say
What was on your mind.
Oh, how I hated the time you made me
Snap those peas.
These days, I could snap
A thousand peas, if you were here.
I wish I could have spent more time
Not thinking in my mind
What you would have said,
And I dread the day
When I, too, must go.
Will they speak to me,
Or will their minds
Be empty like mine was?
Your history
Will forever be a mystery to me,
And it hurts.
Love does hurt,
When you can't go back
And change those few moments.

MOTHER, OH MOTHER

Mother, oh, Mother:
How thankful I am
For you gave birth to me
And raised me to be the man I am today.
For this, I am eternally in your debt.
Mother, oh, Mother:
Forgive me for all the pain I caused you in the past,
For I forgot that, without you,
I would not be,
And, believe me,
I shall never forget again.
Mother, oh, Mother:
You are truly blessed,
For your strength is my strength,
And your love is something I'll ensure
That you never regret.
Mother, oh, Mother:
Let God be
Forever with you,
For, unlike the sun,
The love of God shall never set.

A POET'S WORLD

I am the writing on the paper:
"Those who can't understand my words,
Can't understand me,"
For the words play a different role
Than what they claim to be.
Understand, though,
Despite complexity,
They still represent you
And represent me.

So, what you read
Is not necessarily what you get,
But what you interpret.
Therefore, a poet's world
Is a world with no limits.

In another man's
Or woman's world,
One might drink away
The pain just to maintain,
But, in a poet's world,
One might write himself
Or herself out of being insane.

There are also those who
May speak of life
As being a sort of game,
So, if you decide to play,
Play it for keeps
And not for the fame,
For someone will always
Try to steal your moment of glory
And – in a poet's world –
It is a whole different story.

So, if you enter this world, then be real.
Choose your words wisely,
Because even those nowadays
Will kill,
A poet's world.

THOUGHTS OF ASIA

One of the first serious relationships I had from junior to senior year of high school was with a girl who I will call Asia. Asia and I were seriously involved, but she later wanted to separate. Her reasons were that her needs weren't being met, she wasn't doing the things that she needed to do, and she wasn't happy. Back then, the concept of meeting your lover's needs and you're having your needs be reciprocated was foreign to me. Due to my selfishness at the time, her needs very likely weren't being met, but, at the time, you couldn't tell me that I wasn't in love. You couldn't warn me of the train wreck that was about to happen in this point in my life. I was in love (insert hearts, fireworks, and butterflies here). Like many heartbroken boys, I had to deal with the fact that my so-called "love" no longer loved me.

Asia's new relationship was with an older guy who was known to be a "player." In my mind, Asia was meant for me, but, at the time, you couldn't tell me anything. She was intelligent, and I always thought she looked like a darker and younger Debbi Morgan. The connection I thought we had was unbreakable. She shared painful episodes in her life with me that I thought no other man knew. I always thought I had a special place in her heart; I later learned that her story went around a few times. We were both proactive in organizations and cultural events. She was my "soul sister" or so I thought. And, now, she was with this guy who probably wouldn't be caught dead at a poetry event or a lecture about empowering the African-American community.

My intuition told me that I had to move on, but my insides were getting stabbed repeatedly. Friends thought I was investing too much time in someone who was manipulating my emotions like a master puppeteer. We would go on for a few years looking for something that wasn't there, reaching for something that we could never obtain. I would daydream for hours thinking about us getting back together. Maybe it worked for moments, but nothing manifested. Looking back on the whole thing, I was very young and had no clue about the opposite sex. This may be a little one-sided, but she is neither writing this book with me nor am I in trouble for legal issues since I "changed the names to protect the innocent." Anyway, this is what was going through my mind, for better or for worse.

LOVE AT FIRST SIGHT

I love the sweet soulful sounds
Of harmonious hormones at the peak of ecstasy.
My mind is envisioning erotic episodes
Of the woman standing next to me.
Is it her beautiful brown borders that are the source
Of my affection,
Or am I placing too much emphasis
On my obelisk resurrection?
I must be careful not to make my –
Lustful love-making looks make her uneasy,
For my mission is not to make a booty call
Bounce or boast about how this woman pleased me.
Oh, no!

It's more like wanting worthwhile experiences
With this erotic creature.
Knowing nothing of her nature,
I continue to probe her feminine features.
I tell you, her eyes got me caught up
In a condition of confusion
And it's got to be her that makes me feel this way –
Not some illusion.
[Lord please don't wake me now!]

Her skin is a silky silhouette
Of a dark brown hue,
And, as she stands there seductively,
I don't have a clue what to do.
You see, I am motionless in this mystifying moment,
And I guess you can call me Mike Tyson right now,
For I am overwhelmed by my worthy opponent.

I swear to you,
I have never seen lips look quite like that,
So I am wondering if it is feasible to approach her
With my feelings intact.
If I miss out on this opportunity,
I'll be the only one to blame,
So I walk up to her,
Clear my throat, and say:

"Hi, my name is James, and what is your name?"

Love at first sight.

UNEARTHLY

Where does a woman like you originate?
Do you walk with the wind,
Or do you come down to the Earth
Like the rays of the Sun?
Are you a figment of my imagination,
Or just a vision of what I desire –
A godly creation?

What is your secret?
Do you have a past?
Where do you keep it?
What spell have you cast?
What is the world behind your eyes?
If I'm not seeing the real you,
Where does the truth lie?
Are you the one sent for me,
Or am I wasting my time
With someone else's matrimony?

Are you the black dove sent from above,
Or do you have something to give –
That four–letter word called "love?"
Are you from another place,
Or do you exist only in my mind,
Beyond time and space?

If you are true beauty,
Where do you reside?
If it is heaven,
Can I come inside?
Will you be by my side,
Or are you here only for a visit?
Are you an angel?
Nothing on this earth
Is that exquisite.

THE DREAMER

I have nothing but a dream,
A dream that with each passing day,
Will not be achieved,
A longing to hold onto the past
In fear of losing a blessed future with you,
Loving you.
Many nights, I find myself lost in this dream
To have you once again,
To forget the wrongs we committed in the past
And live for today,
But that dream is not reality.

So, I continue dreaming,
Dreaming to one day be your black knight again
And sweep you off your feet,
To be the one who will lead you
From the beast who threatens you,
The one who threatens our future
The one who *abused* you,
Not made love to you,
But that dream is not reality.
What is reality?
Well,
Reality is without you.
Reality is what I refuse to face because of my heart
Is with you, but you are with –
The other.

So, I continue to dream
A dream in paradise,
Experiencing your inner world,
A dream to once again bond with you,
To dwell in the garden from within
And share your deepest secrets,
But it's only a dream,

So I lie here,
Alone without you,
Living in this world of fantasy,
But fearing losing you forever.
I'm holding on to the only thing that I have left,
But it's not reality.
I can only be –
The dreamer.

TIME

It seems as if she came to me in a dream
Guided by forces unknown or unseen.
My life was hectic.
Hers was serene.
She said that I should stop eating meat
And replace it with more greens
(And she was right),
But it's so easy to do wrong.
She knew where she was when I was finding
Where I belonged.

It hasn't been long since we first met.
She dazzled me
With her high-tech dialect and intellect.
She made my mind and penis erect.
As I reflect on days when we were alone,
As our bodies,
        Minds,
        And souls
Traveled to sacred homes.

We massage each other's mental
To the point of orgasmic vibrations,
Discussing everything from creation
To worldly frustrations.

You see, to me she was God-sent,
So I guess the Devil is responsible
For where she went:
Somewhere where I am not
And where she doesn't want to be.

She left me with a life that was empty,
Only to be filled again.
The only questions are "with whom" and "when?"

Time is where the healing begins.

TOMORROW

Will you remember me when the smoke clears,
And I am the one standing near your heart,
Or will you forget what we started?
Will you remember me
When I am all the man you need,
Or will you let your love rot like an apple
Who never got a chance to sew its seed?
Will you remember how the mere sound of my voice
Made you feel,
Or will someone else steal my flame,
Another name to replace mine?
Will you still be there
When time becomes ripe?
Will you still love me like before,
Or will you want something else?
Will you need something else,
Something more?
Will you remember the passion you felt,
Or will your heart melt forever?
Never knowing the me, to be,
Will there be a tomorrow?
Could there be a tomorrow,
A tomorrow for you and me?

THE DREAMER II (TIME TO WAKE UP)

Forget the dream!
I want to see the dream go up in flames,
And I am to blame for being so naïve.
You tried to deceive me into thinking
That you loved me,
But, like a punk,
You just shoved me from behind,
And had me losing my mind over you.

Don't call me your "boo,"
Or, even, your "baby,"
Cause you will never be my lady again.
Let's not pretend this is the last time
You will use me as your safety net.
To tell you the truth,
I even regret the sex.
You're damn right I'm vexed.

You had me wasting my time
Writing verses and rhymes
About our so-called "love affair."
You don't care about me.
You just don't want to feel lonely,
Night after night.
You only call me when you want something.
You know that ain't right!

But, like a fool, I went to your get-togethers
And did whatever made you happy,
When deep inside, I felt crappy.
Not anymore.
Out of all the apples that I had,
You're rotten to the core,
And I don't have time for the snakes.
I think it's time to get yourself together
Well, at least for your own sake
Because you don't have to do anything for me.
You said you would love me forever,
But that was only a fallacy.
You see, I was once a dreamer
But I had to wake up to reality.

GOOD RIDDANCE

I bought this woman
Candy and flowers,
Ate out for dinner,
And talked for hours,
But it still wasn't enough for her.
She wanted the whole nine yards
When I could only give her seven.
Seven days out of the month?
She wanted eleven.

And life for her and me
Was on a silver platter.
She wanted diamonds.
I said, "When my pockets are 'phatter,'
Because now they're flatter than a pancake."
She said I was being too cheap,
But you can't turn a puddle into a lake
(At least not overnight).
I wanted to compromise.
She wanted to fuss and fight.

It seems like I am cursed,
When it comes to relationships.
I treated her like a queen,
But she would rather be treated like crap,
And that's how it was with her and her ex.
Sometimes I wanted to relax,

But all she wanted was the sex.
Complex things
Seem to happen to simplistic people.
She was fine with the way things were going.
I thought things weren't equal.
Is there a sequel to this madness?
Can you guess?
Just like all things,
This relationship had to end.
She pulled the last straw
When she said,
"I can no longer hang with my friends."
I guess that is my dilemma summed up in a nutshell.
She told me to go to hell.
I just laughed, and said,
"I bid you farewell."

Good riddance!

ANOTHER LOVE POEM

This is not another love poem
Because love only lives
In hearts willing to accept it.
I used to know the feeling.
Now I know not.

Beauty?
Life is ugly as I see it,
Painted with heartbreaks and heartaches.
My heart aches from heart attacks
From past relationships.

I don't write love poems anymore
I write on dark subjects of dark days
Which once were lit brightly.
It's hard to love in a world filled with hate.
Is there someone in my fate?
I guess not,
Because all I see is loneliness.

MORE THOUGHTS OF ASIA

Remember that scene in that movie Boomerang, where Marcus was speaking to Angela on the couch sulking after Jacqueline broke his heart. Who can forget what he said?

"I just want to sit at home, stare at the wall, and listen to Sade."

Let's just say, during this segment of my life, I played Sade until the CDs started skipping. To this day, she is one my favorite artists of all time. Why? Because she can sing your pain in a thousand different ways until you forget you even had pain in the first place. It was only a matter of time until I would pen a poem in her honor.

This is one of my favorite storytelling pieces, for it really challenged me as a writer. Before this poem, most of my pieces would come out as effortlessly as water cascading over a cliff. There was some real thought put into every line, for almost every line is the title of a Sade song. Some lines have a title or two in them. It is through these song titles that I paint a picture of the love-lost story that encompassed most of my high school years. Yep, Asia did a number on me, but Sade freed me until her music stopped.

Challenge yourself, and see if you can pick out all the song titles. And, by the way, don't use the internet to cheat.

I GOT THIS BLUES WHILE LISTENING TO A SADE CD

What we had was no ordinary love.
It was the sweetest taboo –
Paradise.
And, you know what they say:
It is never as good as the first time.
You haunt me,
And I can't pretend
That I feel no pain
Because love is stronger than pride,
But you want to give it up
Instead of hanging on to your love.

Is it a crime to cherish the day
You gave me the kiss of life?
For you are lovers rock,
But you want *me* to keep looking
For just another smooth operator
Named Sally
Or Maureen
To be my cherry pie
When it was all about our love.

Why should I turn my back on you?
Why can't we be together?
For I will always be by your side,
Even though I am feeling like
I am the king of sorrow.

I never thought I'd see the day,

For I thought nothing could come between us,

And now I write this poem

Hanging on to every word,

Hurt, but I have a bulletproof soul.

So with a clean heart

I will clean the mess that I made.

Maybe I *was* Mr. Wrong,

But, now,

Right this minute,

I will be your friend.

1-8-5

1-8-5 was like heaven all over again,
For I have been with someone special.
Even though our paths met before,
It was nice to have another chance to explore
The secrets that Victoria kept hidden,
And words cannot express how I felt
As we caressed,
Making the night the best it has been
In a long time.
As our bodies intertwined,
My mind traveled to the first time we met.
1-8-5 is a place I will never forget.

I never thought I would be
At 1-8-5 as we
We're being serenaded by Will Downing tunes,
Feeling soft lips,
Fingertips
And smelling the aroma of incense fumes.
Our hearts danced,
Complementing our heavy breathing
And seething
For another chance to recapture the past,
Hoping that 1-8-5
Wouldn't be our last.

As it stands,
1-8-5 commands me
To hold onto time's apparatus,
So my status is unknown,
But I have grown to accept
Whatever may be,
For it was more than the physical.
At 1-8-5, I left a piece of me –
1-8-5.

I REMEMBER THE EARTH AND THE MOON

I remember when the Earth
And the moon were one,
And the Sun was the source of life,
And life was filled with love –
Love borne of their unity
And their devotion –
But the unity broke,
And the sun's light dimmed,
But the love didn't end;
It merely transformed.

And the Earth became dark
And lonely, for it needed the moon.
It needed that devotion.
And the moon was still felt, for it moved the oceans
And illuminated
The darkness,
So the Earth yearned for the moon,
For she gave him confidence,
And made him feel loved for even planets
Need to feel appreciated.
They need to feel that closeness with a moon
That is worthy

The moon gives him a bit of happiness
In a universe filled with
>
> Pain,
>
> Hurt,
>
> No–tomorrow
>
> And nowhere.

The Earth will always care for the moon,
Even when she isn't there
Or doesn't feel the way that he does.
I remember what the Earth
And the Moon were
And what they are now,
And I will always remember in the future,
For the Earth is within me,
And the moon will always be she.
I remember,
But will she?

THOUGHTS OF INTROSPECTION

There is an old proverb that says "the eyes are the windows to the soul." Of course, you can't look into someone's eyes and see whether they have the soul of the darkest demon from Hell, but the eyes are the only barriers that separate us from each other's thoughts. Imagine if you can know another person's thoughts. Two things would happen: You would either be a paranoid person, from all the sinister things people think (I am working on all my evil thoughts every day), or be a very rich person from knowing a lot of people's dirty laundry. I'm not pessimistic; I just know how flawed we all are, myself included.

An experiment has been conducted in which brain scans were performed on test subjects after they were required to look at pictures of faces. The researcher programmed the computer that was scanning their brains to determine their reaction to each face. Thus, the computer correlated each reaction to a particular face. It wasn't quite mind-reading, but this development could lead to that very outcome. [3] *Is it me, or does this sound like this is right out of the script of a Sci-Fi movie?*

---

[3] Weintraub, Karen. "Scientists Explore Possibilities of Mind Reading." *USA TODAY* 22 Apr. 2014. Web. 18 Dec. 2014.
<http://www.usatoday.com/story/tech/2014/04/22/mind-reading-brain-scans/7747831/>.

Believe me, the next group of poems is not going in that direction; I'm just channeling my inner nerd again.

My point is, we might see devices that can actually come very close to reading your thoughts. For now, we can only go by people's body language. Physical reactions don't always line up with the way people feel. We can only make assumptions based on a track record. In a sense, we are blinded to the world inside each and every one of us. In fact, the whole reason for me writing these poems are to expose the world inside of me. This is my reason for taking you on this journey, but you can only get there through My Eyes. They are the way to my feelings.

MY EYES

You find yourself lost in my eyes,
Taking you to undiscovered places.
You try to probe my thoughts,
But my eyes, dark irises,
Compel you to me,
Filling you with bewilderment
And enchanting you with my spell.

Let me take you on a journey
Through my eyes,
Away from the world
As you know it,
Bringing you through Hell
And, then, into paradise –
Experiencing sadness,
Then giving you joy.

Through my eyes,
You will find many levels:
Those of love,
Those of desire,
Those of compassion,
And those of fire.
Look into my eyes,
And experience what I see.
Let me take you on an escapade
To the world inside of me.

CRIES OF A WOMAN

The slight sound of a woman's heartbeat is heard,
Adding to the sounds around her.
Beads of sweat fill her eyebrows,
Dripping down the side of her face.
Her body is tense as she feels violent motions
Between her legs.

Tears formulate as the motion persists.
I hear her there, crying out for God,
Which echoes through my ears.
Her breathing is heavy,
Like the breathing of her deepest fears.

She screams again,
Hoping that someone can relieve her pain,
But no immediate response is met,
So she lays there on her back as this action persists,
Hoping that her pain will cease to exist.

She cries out again –
The motion becomes amplified –
More and more sweat trickles down her face.

She lets out one last cry
When the motion ceases to exist.
A voice is heard.
She looks toward her legs.

"It's a boy!"

Words suddenly break the silence.
A sudden joy is felt as the woman smiles.
The doctor puts the baby boy in her hands.
She kisses the baby,
    Cries,
    And, then, says

"Oh, Father...You have another son."

THE MAD POET

You don't know me.
I don't know you.
I'm just a face behind the lights
Separated by this steel mic,
But that's all right with me.
I like the fact that after hearing my poetry,
You think you know me,
But you don't.
In fact, the part of me that was in the poem,
You missed.
Now, check this!

Does a poet write for your ears,
Or is a poet's words heard even when you don't hear?
You see, a poet is a poet even if there's no crowd,
And despite how loud you applaud,
So if you write for the people,
And call yourself a poet then you're a fraud.
That's what a wise man once said,
But it's a shame you don't recognize a good poet
Until he or she is dead.

Think:
How many poets can you count in your membrane?
Don't even bother, because most of you
Can't even remember my name.
You see, I represent the real writers

(Even the ones who don't even know it),
Not the fakes stealing lines from other artists,
And calling themselves poets.
They get on an open mic just to get an orgasm,
But, if you share a stage with me,
You'll catch a tongue spasm,
And someone will ask:

"Are those your lines?"

Now you're shook,
And half of you out there
Never even picked up a book by
   Nikki Giovanni,
   Sonia Sanchez,
   Or David Walker.
And don't smile,
Because most of you
Will listen to any good talker.

You know what I'm talking about:
The type who tries to make
A whole lot of nothing into something,
When basically all they are doing is bluffing.
That's the breaks, I guess.
I think I'll coin a new term:

Poet–less!

Less than a poet
How's that for linguistics?
Nothing fancy –
Something simplistic,
Because if it was up to me,
All of you fake poets' pens would be broken.
It's a new day,
And the mad poet has spoken.

THE GREAT O' US OF A

While the rich play poly-tics,
Cops play poly tricks with nightsticks.
Living in the bricks there's no peace.
Can I get a piece?
Man, can u give me a piece of that artificial pie?
Our people get high on philosophical lies,
So what fallacies are you smoking today?

Do you know where your children are?
I do!
They travel far from morals,
Dying like coral reefs with no chiefs
And no beliefs to follow.
Black minds are being swallowed.
In corporate America –
Land of the free and home of the brave –
Our children are being put
In Special Ed. because they can't "behave."

And where are the brave souls –
Bought and sold by IBM or AT&T?
Those who claim they got eyes will never see.
I'm in the middle of two lives:
One that I want to live,
And one I have no choice but to live.
Can I hand you some knowledge that college
Couldn't even give?

Brother, you better know your place.
Brother, you better run that race against time,
Selling nickels and dimes.
Every young black boy wants to play ball or rhyme,
And crime pays.
Crime will have you locked up for days.
In many ways, we're like the projects.
I've seen some of the greatest intellects turn to rejects.
Line up to get your welfare checks!
Line up if you're the prime suspect
In the Central Park shooting!

Our people are looting their own neighborhoods.
Sisters are up to no good,
Having sex like it's a sport
And selling their souls into slavery
Like slave ports.

This society seems more concerned with Bill Clinton
And Monica Lewinski than with police brutality.
If the Devil was a human being,
Then I guess it's Giuliani –
More concerned with Versace and Armani.
They killed our leaders.
Now, they are killing blacks today,
Drugs are still in our communities
Courtesy of the CIA, and racism is here to stay.
Somebody tell me.
There's got to be a better way in the great o' US of A.

MORE THOUGHTS OF INTROSPECTION

A Lost Sheep is a recollection of how I felt at one point in my life. I came to the realization that, in my life, there was nothing but emptiness. I didn't know my purpose. What was I meant to do? Would I ever be successful? Fear and distractions – weapons of the Devil – get in the way of reconnecting us with whom God intended us to be.

Financial guru Dave Ramsey said it best:

"You are never too old. You are never the wrong color. You are never too disabled. You are never the wrong political party. There is never a big enough obstacle to keep a person with passion operating in a higher calling from winning."

The truth is we all want to win. In this poem, I draw a parallel between my state of being lost and people of African descent. Going as far back as the days of slavery, African people had the leadership to guide them through their struggles. Of course, I am speaking of when the battle for human rights began for my people. African leadership can be traced as far back as the beginning of time. This leadership would flourish until the end of the Civil Rights era, leading us to current day. Where are the Queen Hatshepsut's, the Toussaint L'Overture's, the Denmark Vesey's, the Nzinga's, the

Stokely Carmichael's, the Medgar Evers's, etc. of today? There are too many to name in one book. This poem is a cry for my savior, and the savior of my people, to rise again.

A LOST SHEEP

A lost sheep
With no direction,
No leadership,
And no one to turn to:
That is what I am.

A lost sheep
Filled with bewilderment,
Filled with pain,
And filled with fear:
That is what has become of me.

A lost sheep
Without Harriet Tubman,
Without Marcus Garvey,
And without Malcolm X:
That's what I have no choice but to be.

A lost sheep
Who must find its way,
Who must lead others,
Whom others must turn to
So they won't be like me.

OUTER SPACE IN OUTER SPACE

Some say my mind is in outer space.
I say my mind is out of space.
Space and time are only mere extensions of this world.

My thoughts contain mysteries like dark matter,
That which is invisible but whose forces interact
With every celestial body.

It's kind of like black people:
Society's dark matter made to be Invisible,
But whose power of influence is felt,
Or like black holes:
        Powerful,
        Unseen,
        And unknown.
Blacks are synonymous with the afterthought
(Or the thought after the afterthought),
Only thought about when someone happens to ask,

"Did you ever think about *them*?"

Some say my mind is in outer space,
But I say my mind is out of space,
Pondering frivolous statements like
"All roads lead to Rome."
It's more like your roads should lead to home,
Because that is where your heart should be.

Kind of like the "Road to Perdition,"
The road to perfection, to realization.
You see, it is nice to put things in perspective.

Some say my mind is in outer space.
I say my mind is out of space.
Space and time only mere extensions of this world.

For instance,
You have to be at such-and-such a place
At such-and-such a time,
But cells are said to change,
Replace themselves,
So who is really at such-and-such a place
At such-and-such a time?
And how would that relate to clones?
If they are replicas of us,
And the only thing that is constant is change,
Then wouldn't that mean your clone wouldn't be
A replica at all,
All your thoughts and instincts a thing of the past?

I know what you are thinking:
I have really lost my marbles.
Well, if madness is close to genius,
Then call me a mad genius.
My mind is out of space
From all the enigmas that I ponder.
I spend most of my time sitting in secluded rooms

And let my mind wonder about things like
The Big Bang Theory –
And that's exactly what it is: just a theory
Which, to this day, has yet to be proven,
Though scientists waste their lives away on it,
Or they spend more time trying to cure cancer
Then the common cold.
I was told that you have to crawl before you walk.

My mind is out of space with thoughts of UFOs
And cornfields and crop circles,
But I'm more scared than Mel Gibson
That a monster will be outside my window;
The monster could be
Right in my bedroom,
Sleeping in the same bed.
And I think of things like
Ancient Khemetic societies,
And how, in "The Mummy,"
Imhotep was made to be the villain,
Though his very name means
"The one that comes in peace,"

Analyzing disturbing human behavior,
And comparing and contrasting
To my own deficiencies.
See I'm in search
For the lies that lie beneath the truth.
Yes, I'm in search of the lies

That lie beneath the truth,
For how can you know the truth without testing it
against the lie?

My mind is out of space because of my third eye
Keeps blinking, thinking of
    People,
    Places
    And things,
But don't turn out the lights,
Because "I see dead people" at night:
People from the past who paved the way for people like
me to live,
Who whispers in my ear that it is time for me to give
That which they already gave.

And, so, it begins when I take all my thoughts
And translate them into actions,
Only taking a fraction of the time
To process in my mind what I write on paper.
Then downloading the excess information
So that I can upload some more,
So my thoughts can have more room,
More memory, but you still think
My mind is in outer space.
You still think I am out of place
When maybe it is your mind that has *too* much space
And not thoughts to fill it with.

CHAPTER 2: SUCKED IN AND TORN APART

Like I said earlier, I had no clue about the opposite sex. I promise you I do recover towards the end. It was a long road though. At this moment in my life, I was trying to mend pieces of my soul with my vices, magnifying my flaws to uncharted levels. Emotionally, I was hurting but masked it with my defense mechanisms. The black hole of my life had pulled me in, and it was now pulling me apart. I guess you can say I was going to hell in a handbag.

This is the part of the book in which I have to apologize to my mother in advance. Yes, Mom, your son wasn't a golden boy at all. But, something tells me that she might have had an inkling as to what was going on. Nevertheless, my mother might have to read ahead a bunch of pages (laughing inside). The rest of you can stay with me; I never lived with any of you, so all of you will be alright. I digress.

It started with the drinking. College parties were introduced to me before the end of my senior year of high school. By this time, my relationship with Asia was a literal blur from all the drinking, but the hole that was left in my soul wasn't being filled. What I failed to mention at the beginning about the Asia relationship was it started out badly in the first place. I was already in another relationship with a girl I will call Ebony.

Things went sour for Ebony and me after rumors that she and a so-called friend of mine had a make-out session at a house party. When I met Asia, it made leaving Ebony much easier, but it certainly wasn't the wisest of decisions. To say I felt nothing for Ebony would be a lie. But, I guess I got everything I deserved from Asia.

Fast-forward a bit. Ebony was truly at the wrong place at the wrong time when I ran into her again at my high-school graduation; she was from another town. To make matters worse, I also ran into another young lady, Ivory, one whom I had a crush during my early high-school days. Yep: I was "ratchet" before there were reality shows. Nothing became of us, though, at the time, she was with a friend of a friend of mine. Being the wreck I was at this point in time, you can see where this road turns. Thus, I started dating both Ebony and Ivory. You can remove the Michael Jackson and Paul McCartney song from your mind.

Getting back to the point, later, while visiting home during college, I got a three-way call that would make even Goldie stutter: Ebony and Ivory on my phone at the same time. When the jig is up, the jig is up. What was I to do, but "fess up" and take my lumps? Unfortunately, it was all downhill from there for years: cheating, womanizing and strip clubs. I was crawling deeper into the hole I had dug for myself. Forget "the good, the bad, and the ugly;" I went from bad to just plain old ugly. When a star gets too close to a black hole and is sucked in, there is nothing left in its future but to be torn apart.

THE PLAYER

I'm caught in a game,
One that I don't want to play,
But that I just can't escape.
Wounded from the past,
I can no longer trust another,
But the eagerness to be loved
Is still within,
So I search from one
To the other,
Wanting to gain what was lost,
But causing hurt to others
Unintentionally,
Misleading,
Deceiving,
Living the life of
The player.

LETTER #1

Dear Ebony and Ivory,
I'm writing this letter knowing you will never see it
And probably will never hear it,
But I am writing it anyway.
I just wanted to say
That I wasn't man enough for you then,
And I can't even begin
To tell you the places
I've been now.

See, when I was with both of you,
I didn't know how to love.
Instead, I was thinking of
What I could get out of the situation.
It wasn't out of sexual frustration.
It was more like a love fixation that I had in the past,
And time moves fast as I realize
The type of women that I was dealing with.

Just like a permanent scar,
What I've done in the past will remain,
And it pains me to think of all the trouble I caused.
Because I was blind to your greatness,
I know it would be hard for both of you to take this
Letter that I write sincerely.

Now, I see clearly that it was my loss
And that I ended friendships at my own cost.
I will forever wonder what could have been.
If I could turn back the hands of time,
Even though that power is not mine.
I would.
Now, I will love one
And won't love another,
And will be the best man I can—
Not that I could.

Sincerely,
James C. Ellerbe

WILL YOU SEE LOVE

Will you see me?
Will you see me amongst scattered dreams,
Where life is nothing but multi-colored dreams
Colliding with nightmares at high speeds.
Where time is a foreign concept,
And all your precepts are connected to a single frame,
Like the movie of your mind?
It is there you will find me,
But will you see me?

Will you be able to reach out and touch
A mere shadow of your expectations
For a lesser creation, a higher soul –
Who traveled through a black hole
To reach your dimension?
This is no Twilight Zone.
Consider me the beacon calling you home
So your soul can roam with me for a while.
We can sail down the Nile a million miles away.
That way, it will take even longer to return
To the place of origin.
Soaring beyond the Earth's gravitational pull,
Because space Is where stars are born
Because this space without you is where scars
Are torn to pieces,
I would rather be worn like the creases in your jeans
So you will know what it means to be together.

Will you see me —just for a second or two?
Will you let me get next to you
And take this moment with you always
So that all your days and nights will never be alone?

Will you hear me in the sultry tones
Of N'Dea Davenport,
Inhale me like a Newport,
And give an in-depth report
To your friends and colleagues
Of how you swam through oceans,
One thousand leagues of ecstasy?
I want you right here next to me,
But will you see me?
Will you see love?

TIME (PART 2: SCORN AGAIN)

I can close my eyes and envision you
But not the real you:
A surreal you,
But unlike you.

Your memory is forever unchanged,
The same as it was before,
Something that I can count on to show up
When the rains come.
Our hearts are worlds apart like the Bering Strait:
You are one continent,
I, the other, and your man is the ocean.
For this, our souls are separated by time.

My mind fantasizes about one day when our worlds
Are no longer worlds away from each other.
The ocean is no longer the space between us,
And thus, we are hand-in-hand,
Woman to man, our future, unknown.

But, I have grown to face what is and what is not –
Just a faded dream,
So, it seems this is the way it was meant to be:
A life and space left empty,
But a friendship born.
Time has left me scorned again.

YOU DON'T LOVE ME; YOU LOVE MY POETRY,

the way it comforts your insecurities
To the point where you can live again,
'Til you can give again,
Give the love that should've been there
In the first place –to erase what you really feel.
It makes the wheels in your head turn.
It burns bridges and takes the ridges out of life.
It makes you see past all this strife.

You don't love me;
You love the way the words sound,
How they resonate in your cerebral cavity,
How my pen defies gravity
(For I will never put it down),
And how it transcends the bounds
Of your own town
To a whole new perception.
It arouses your intellect,
Giving you something to reflect on.
Word is born!

You don't love me;
You love the poet inside of me,
How the words make you want to ride me,
Let the verses just bust up inside thee
To the point where you need a cigarette,
How they make you forget you even have a man

And change your plans to hear me recite.
You don't love me;
You love the way that I write and would give anything
To have my poems in your life.

My words give you something
To chase the ghosts away and, on a rainy day,
They even make the sun come out to play.
Now, as you can see,
It is easy to love me,
But, in order to love me,
You've got to first
Love
My poetry.

A PLACE CALLED ALONE

Alone.
Home seems so far away, so I stray
To uncharted territory
Hoping that I don't end up in Alone again.
See, alone is a place not too far from the state I am in.
2 blocks and I am back there again,
On that same track again,
Hoping that, maybe, this time, the train will derail.
I fail to see the point of going back to that place called
Alone.
Its population is
Me,
Myself
And I.
I hope I don't die there.
This place has many stories.
I live in a building with 1,000 stories of tears.
Damn! It seems like I've been in there for years.
I need a change of scene.
I want to know what it means to be not at Alone,
But I'm thrown into this place.
I have grown into this space.
But, I must escape from Alone.

I KNEW I WAS IN TROUBLE

I knew I was in trouble when I first saw you.
I tried to double back,
But my mind couldn't seem to turn the other way.
I must say, you were a sight to behold,
As if you were the coal compressed a thousand-fold
To make a diamond, ten units above platinum.
I try to shun the thought of how it would taste
To place my lips upon yours,
Since a kiss from you would start a Trojan War
Inside of me and all around me.
I have to shake my head to ground me,
For your presence is the essence of sensuality.
Your physicality is beyond reality.
It's as if you were genetically engineered for me,
Like you are the feminine reincarnation of me.
I know I am in trouble now
Because trouble has found me,
So I try to look away.
I try to run away,
But the thought still stays,
For I know that, if I could,
I would have you in every way.

CONTEMPLATION

It seems like she spent a lifetime
In my mind,
Spinning and falling in love,
Which lives in me,
So I began to touch her,
Slowly, like a flick in slow motion.
She was my potion, so I sipped her.
She was my black hole,
So I dipped her
And unzipped her inner emotions.

I swam through her ocean
Over
And
Over
Again.
Her ocean slammed against my rocks
Over
And
Over
Again
With so much force,
And so much passion,
So much force
In multiple fashions.
I'm asking for this to never end,
And I could see a thousand reverends,

But I would still intend
To be inside of her.

Do you mind if I tell you more?
How I explored her Congo
And played her bongos 'til dawn?
I was born,
Then reborn
And spawned inside of her,
A flower that bloomed.
We both saw the Sun,
The moon and the stars,
And we traveled to Mars in one breath.
Let me stop lying;
Numerous breaths left
My chest cavity,
And gravity brought us down to Earth,
Only to give birth to another dimension.

Did I mention how beautiful the night ended,
How we traveled on bridges we once thought
Were broken and heard words
That need not have been spoken,
But which were said anyway?
I wish I had you every day,
But I can't,
And now my head has found peace,
And all the pain of the past
Can now be released,

Gone from whence it came –
Like a forgotten name
And number.
Cumbersome, she is not.
Love was felt inside of her,
Not tainted like a dirty street
Or a run-down block,
For heaven wasn't just between her thighs –
Heaven was behind her eyes.
I heard heaven entrenched in her cries,
For she felt beautiful,
And that was suitable for my happiness.

I guess it was meant to be.
I guess she was meant for me.
I guess she is matrimony.
I want us to do like lovers do,
And make love from Sunday to Saturday.
Shouldn't love be this way?
Shouldn't love feel this way?
Shouldn't love be the only way?

COMPUTER LUV

We made love without touching.
The blood rushing to my phallus
Like water over the levees in New Orleans,
It seems like I can be with her forever in my mind.
Time is nonexistent.
Listening to every word typed –
Might be taboo,
But it helps me get through
And makes me feel whole again.
Exciting like original sin,
I don't know when this happened,
But it was meant to be.
Two minds exploring each other like biology
I envision her astrology with every curve mapped out
Until the energy is zapped out of me.
Like an all-night orgy,
But she is not in front of me
She is behind a computer screen, but it seems so real.
Oh, the way she makes me feel.

NOT WORTHY

You look into my eyes
Searching for my soul,
So I let your quest continue,
But I think to myself
"I'm not worthy,"
And this is true.

I look into your soul
And nothing that comes from me
Could be as beautiful as you,
Could be as good as you.
You are the sweetest of sweets,
So our souls could never meet.

But I envision anyway.
I wish that, on any day,
I could be the paintbrush
To your canvas,
And I can't stand this,
But I know that I'm not worthy.

You could have a thousand men
Better than I,
But you choose me to be by your side.
You are the highest of high,
And rock bottom is where I reside,
So I realize that I'm not worthy.

But I can't dismiss
The feeling of wanting one kiss
From the lips that sailed 1,000 ships
And cause lunar eclipses,
But I'm not worthy,
And I understand,
So I fantasize about you
Taking my hand
And lead me to paradise,
But I'm not worthy,
So only my thoughts can suffice.

JUST WHAT

What do you do when there's
No more conversations
Between the physical explorations
When there's nothing but silence
And blank faces
And no traces of intelligence
Where nothing said is relevant
In the situation at hand
When the sex is minimal
Only replaced by subliminal messages?
Like

"Not tonight...I'm tired honey!"

What do you do
When the jokes are no longer funny
But offensive
And got you on the defensive
To the point when you shout...

"What was all that about?!"

What do you do
When you can't stand to be in the same space,
When you are tired of the same face
Looking through you,
Not at you?

What do you do when he or she has had enough
When he or she is packing their stuff
To go live at a friend's house?

What do you do
When he or she doesn't act like your spouse
And doesn't open his or her mouth anymore?

What else can be done
When you no longer have fun,
When you are no longer the one whom he desires
Or no longer the one to light her fire?

What do you do at the end
When you can't be friends,
When you can no longer pretend
The relationship was worth it?

What can you do?
What can be done?
What do you do at the end?

Nothing.

MONOGAMOUS

I think I lost you somewhere in a dream.
Something is not what it seems,
As if my definition is not what it means
And I'm struggling to see what lies beneath,
But I'm not Harrison Ford,
So something had to seep through,
Like something leaked through
The fabric of our relationship.

Monogamy
Turning the lust into a minus
And, trust me, it's not easy.
It just means the
The temptation will always be there,
Only hidden.

Was expressing my feelings
Unforgiving,
An original sin?
When is it safe, then?
Do the floodgates ever open?

We were coasting.
Now, something put on the brakes,
Or I must have never taken your breath away,
Or at least not the way you took mine.
I want to find your heart

I want to start something,
But my back is against the wall,
Only for my feelings to crawl in a corner
And become idle.
Sometimes, just hearing your voice
Is vital to my survival.
Are you, too, complex?
Are you *too* complex,
And, I, too primal?

TIME, TIME, TIME

The one thing that I truly hate about life –
Is time.
Everything consists of time
Like, she can't go out on a date
Because she doesn't have "the time."
She should have said,

**"Why should I waste my time
On someone like you?"**

We tend to relate time to all types
Of stupid stuff like:

"Funny how time flies when you're having fun."

I don't see anything "fun" about that.
If you were having fun,
Wouldn't you want it to last
And not be a thing of the past?
Or, here is a classic:

"OK, it's time for me to go."

No, it is time that I
Leave your lame butt
Because I can think of better things to do
With my time.

You've got to excuse me,
But I just hate that word "time,"
Or anything that has time in it,
Like:

"Better luck next time,"

Or

"Do you have the time?"

Yes, I do,
But I don't plan on giving it to you.
How about this one?

"Time is on my side."

Man!
Time has never been on my side.
Time has been kicking the crap out of me
I just want to put Time in a headlock
And slam Time to the floor.
Stomp the dog mess out of Time
'Til it can't take any more

I know I'm getting a little beside myself
But Time started it
Time has been winning since the beginning –
Of time

(Whenever that is)
Because we are the ones who created it
In the first place.
It's more like we have created a monster
And, above all things,
The number one statement that I hate
Containing time is

"I guess I see you next lifetime."

More like never,
Because that is exactly what a lifetime is.
Time could kiss my butt!

NOMAD IN NO-MANS-LAND

Time keeps slip sliding away like payday,
And no one seems to hear my cries for mayday,
So I wait for Isis to resurrect my soul from this crisis.
They say life is priceless,
But it keeps sticking me in the butt like thorns.
My people tell me I was destined for greatness,
But I've been damned since the day I was born.

"So I keep...holding on!"

To loosely knitted dreams that seem intangible,
For life won't let you take on more than you can
handle,
And I can light a candle for every lesson not learned.
Like a glass of gin and tonic, the truth bums my throat,
But I must cope with reality.
I am trying to do right in this world,
But these devils keep on battling me,
Systematically breaking me down to nothingness,
Consumed with stress
As I go from having a job to joblessness,
Because life is like the roulette table
And I don't think I'm able to keep my head above
water.
Sometimes I think I ought to pull the trigger.
I tell my wife I am trying,
But all she sees is another shiftless ...

Go figure.

It seems the more I keep wasting my time,
The more I keep losing my mind
Trying to find the days I never had.
Whoever thought life would be this bad?
Call me a nomad
In no-man's-land
Going nowhere fast,
Crying out to God

"Oh, I hope this pain won't last?"
"What have I done to make all this misfortune come to past?"

I'm waiting for the Ravens to rock me to sleep.
Call me a nomad in no-mans-land.
I pray the Lord my soul to keep.

WHAT A SONG CAN DO

We are listening to Robin Thicke,
And you slowly slip into my mind.
I'm kissing you from behind your neck,
Rubbing your shoulders
And trying hard not to go over the limit,
But inside, I'm begging you to give it
So I could let you know what it's like to make music –
to live it.

I'm feeling like time is irrelevant,
Overwhelmed by your benevolence
Wanting to take your love and hide the evidence
So you won't feel any regrets.

Let's foreplay 'til the day grows old
(Only if you're bold and you can hold on
Just long enough to be satisfied).
I'll try not to sneak a peek inside,
But if I do, let me slide and glide in you so smooth
That your body feels
Like it's getting maintenance from Jiffy Lube,
Hold you so tight that you feel like I'm glued to you.
It's amazing what one song will do to you:
Because shockwaves to travel through you
And electrify then intensify
To the point at which you identify with your inner
deity.

Let your inner deity connect with me
Like your name is Mary
From Octavia Butler's *Mind of My Mind*
Trapped in your pattern
And, now, our powers combine.

Let time be our factor.
Let me calculate the angles
Of your sensations like a protractor.
Be the explorer who finds the Holy Grail.
Unveil your secret universe,
Release your curse
And turn your worst fears into reverse.

Be the beginning of that cataclysmic event.
Be the portal to places you never went.
Make you're spent words unspent.
Let every curve on your body know that it is special.
I know I'm not worthy of your temple.
I just want you to know
What goes on inside of this mental
So you can understand what I feel.

Let me kneel between your legs
And peel off your covering to reveal your passion fruit.
You don't have to refute this.
You don't have to mute your bliss.
Take these words and treat them like a kiss
Until the sensation runs through you.

It's amazing what a song will do.

WHAT A DANCE WILL DO

Time is like a virus spreading too fast,
But we slow it down as we lock iris to iris,
Soul II Soul.
The beat skips,
But we

"Keep on moving...don't stop like the hands of time,"

And I'm smiling
Because I got you on my mind,
Lost in every grind,
Intertwined in my arms,
Reaching for your palms to feel your pulse.

We dance closely,
But are worlds apart.
We dance close, like heart to heart,
Hoping the song never ends.
I'm feeling your vibe again and again,
Mending the past,
Hoping that this dance surpasses what was
And opens the door to what is,
Forgetting about what he or she did
Because it's us now.
I can't lie: I am lost in your smile,
Lost in your groove,
Hoping that the person next to me will

"Move! Get out the way, get out the way"

Because what we have
Is better than a day at the beach,
And, now, I can't get enough of Ms. Georgia Peach.
I just want to reach into your soul,
Hold you forever,
Weather all of your storms
And unite our worlds mentally
'Til the physical gets jealous
And wants to feel what the mind sees.
When you are with me,
I want to put your mind at ease,
And I will do everything in my power to please you.
It is truly amazing what a dance will do.

THOUGHTS OF THE WORDS

From the late '90s until the early 2000s, there was a trend going on in the spoken-word genre. It was around this period that HBO aired "Def Poetry Jam" for 5 seasons, and everyone who dared to pick up a pen was trying to sound like the last person that they heard on an open mic.

Men and women would rise from their seats to perform sexually vulgar lyrics, make them rhyme and call that poetry. Nevermind trying to get on stage and recite something special or so inspiring that it would cause men and woman to want to go home and begin to move mountains. No! There was not one thought of whether they left some serious, thought-provoking content on that stage. Oh, no! Now, don't get me wrong: I do not "hate" on erotic poetry – not at all.

Erotic poetry can simultaneously be very beautiful and profound. It can elicit longing and yearning for the purest expression of love, or cause the listener to look at love-making from a whole different perspective. It is soothingly creative. If you get a chance, read the Song of Solomon in the Holy Bible; some of the most beautiful erotic poetry of all time is in that book. There is a big difference between erotic poetry and vulgar poetry. One is artistic, and the other is crude and offensive, lacking any substance at all.

This was the inspiration for the poem "Poems for P," which I wrote after hearing so many male poets recite their versions of "erotic poetry." I was tired of going to open mics and hearing the same type of unpoetic blurbs of what people were trying to pass off as erotic poetry. Even in that time period, when I was on my downward spiral, I still knew the difference between art and crap. Mentally, I was screwed up, but poetry seemed to keep me from completely falling off of the cliff.

POEMS FOR P

He trades poems for the P
Like stocks on the stock market,
Lacing lyrics with sexual content about
Time never spent or positions never explored,
Never meeting his own expectations
And never sticking to his own limitations
Of love and romance.

He makes a song and dance
About how he can make women wet and wild.
He's suffering from a mild case of narcissism
Seducing through poetic "gism"
And creating false notions,
Adding ingredients to his potion –
His aphrodisiac, for he lacks the integrity of poetry –
Increasing his potion's potency all in an effort
To get that P.

And it bothers me, for it takes the beauty
Out of words that bring herds of people
Who wish for someone to articulate verbatim
Feelings equal to those of their own
Spheres of understanding,
Demanding that you surpass their everyday lives
And speak words engrossed in their cries,
But he would rather take them on a ride,
For his policy is to get that P by any means necessary.

He's only putting a Band-Aid on the sores
Of a woman's psyche,
Masturbating on paper to his own masquerade
To get laid and parade around like he's some
Casanova.
I should cast his butt over a cliff
And onto a monolith for trying to pawn that malarkey
As poetry for the
  P,
  Punani,
  Nappy dugout,
  Peach,
  Plum.
Most men will do anything to get some,
And poetry is no exception.

He's a mastermind to get that behind
And corrupt minds trapped in time by every line,
I shall rewind.
I said, he is a mastermind to get that behind
And corrupt minds trapped in time
By every line, but the pleasure will be all mine,
For I will expose all poet hoes who uses
Prose and verses as curses.
I should put these poets on the stroll,
Prostitute their behinds
With high-heeled pumps and purses.
You make me sick!!!
Why don't you use your words for something

Besides satisfying your stick!

A LIVING HELL

For the ones who are trying to find a better way, but don't know the way...

Night falls on the chocolate city like a solar eclipse,
Leaving only a glimpse of what is left,
Like a silhouette outlining dark places.
I looked in the mirror and saw the faces
Of black queens that I schemed on.

"Word is born!"

I was dispersed amongst concrete concentration camps
called projects and exchanged food stamps
In order to eat.
I sold "nickels and dimes" just to make ends meet.
I got a little daughter,
So I ought to be ashamed of myself,
But there's no room for regrets.
The rent is due on Friday, so I must not forget.

I lay here on my bed wishing I were dead,
But you know what they say:
You can't get to Heaven that way.

Where I'm from, you get a messed-up education.
It's no wonder why my black tail is still on probation.
The only stimulation I get is when my lips are on a 40,
Sex, or masturbation.
Yes, my mind is trapped on streets

Infested with hood rats who carry gats
And ghetto queens who turn into crack fiends
Asking me for a "dolla."
I feel like Marvin Gaye.

"It just makes me wanna holla!"

The stress got me messing with chicken-heads.
I confess I'm doing wrong,
But my baby's mother and I don't get along,
And around my block, you've got cops
Looking for the next hard rock to harass.
Giving them the finger is just giving them
Another head to bash.
I got a job making little-to-nothing,
While cats are rolling in a Lexus or any latest hot-rod.
It just makes me want to rob them,
But I can't "knock their hustle."

I wake up every morning to roaches in my cereal,
And it's a miracle that I'm still alive
(Or, shall I say, a pity)
Because the streets are gritty,
And I'm just living enough for the city.

My "moms" kicked me out of the house
When I turned twenty,
But it's funny how she won't kick out her man
Who beats the hell out of her every little chance he can.

You look at me as if I am the enemy
When I'm just "tryna" live.
Can't you tell?
You can't judge me unless you walk in my shoes.
If you did, you'd see why my life is a living hell.

I GOT A DATE WITH THE DEVIL

I got a date with the Devil
And I can't be late.
She said to meet her at the local spot
Around eight o' clock,
So I must not make her wait.

I looked in the mirror to make sure I'm nice and neat,
Put a nice shirt on,
And find some shoes to put on my feet,
Spray some cologne on my neck,
Take another glance in the mirror
To make sure I'm straight.
I got a date with the devil,
So I must not be late.

She told me don't think twice
Because she would be there,
And she would never stand me up,
Because she would always be there.

So, here I am, on the corner of Hell Boulevard
Waiting for my date,
And there she was –
Seductive as ever and not a second too late.
We walk into the bar to find a place to sit.
She orders me a Long Island Iced Tea and says,

"Here, now, take a sip.
Take a sip for leaving the woman
Who loved you the most for another
Take a sip for betraying your fellow brother
By dating his baby's mother.
Take a sip for lusting after a married man's wife.
Take a sip for messing up your own life."

The more I sip,
The more she seems right.
And, as I sip some more, this date feels right,
But the night isn't over.
The night has just begun,
This isn't just another date to her,
A soul is to be won and I am the one,
Because I felt all that I had left was her,
And, as I sip on more spirits,
All I see is her.

Now, I am drunk out of my mind
And I can barely stand on my feet.
She says,

"Follow me."

And we make our way out to the street.
She says,

"I can give you something to get by.

Let's get in your car and go for a ride."

The Devil now leads me to a motel,
And it is in this motel
That I am introduced to "Mo" Hell.
She strips down to a matching
Bra and panties set,
And, now, I can feel my manhood swell.
As she takes off all the rest,
I am one step closer to the bowels of Hell.

She smiles and says,

"I know you want me,
And you will have me any way you want me,
But, in order to have me,
You have to first pay me."

And, that, I did.
At that point,
A price was put on my soul,
And I placed my bid.

At the end of the night,
I no longer felt right
And, when I went home and looked in the mirror,
I couldn't bear the sight.
I sold my soul to the Devil,
And that was that.

I sold my soul to the Devil.
Oh, God, please help get my soul back.

CHAPTER 3: BEYOND THE EVENT HORIZON (PARADIGM SHIFT)

During the darkest part of my life, it was like I was two different people: the person God was trying to mold me into, and the person who I wanted to be. But, it's like the Holy Bible says:

"No one can serve two masters. Either you will hate the one and love the other, or you will be devoted to the one and despise the other..." (Matthew 6:24 NIV)

Basically, the light was trying to shine through the darkness. I'm not sure if my friends and peers saw this happening, and, if they did, I'm sure I was confusing the mess out of them. To be honest, I was confusing myself; something had to give. This state can be very destructive to one's well-being.

There is a saying that God is constantly pulling on the hearts of all souls. The question is, do you follow, or do you stay lost in your own world? During this part of my life, the tugging was getting stronger, but the road God was leading me to was scary. Any place where you haven't been before can seem scary. The funny thing is part of the tugging that I mentioned earlier was a passion for something. What do I mean? All of us have a burning to do something in our lives without which we cannot be happy. You won't be happy until you are pursuing your passion, and, until then, you will always think that something is missing. This is proof that God has a plan for all of us and that He bestows gifts and talents on all of us.

There was a shift happening in my life, and it was one I couldn't run from. My perspectives on spirituality, love, and life were beginning to be shaped and sketched into a beautiful tapestry. The close I grew to God, the closer I got to the person He intended me to be. This, by far, is not a finished process, nor is any one of us complete until we have run the race of life. I have a lot of traveling to do and experiences to encounter, but I can only imagine how it will feel at those final moments. This might have been what the apostle Paul was experiencing when he wrote this:

"I have fought the good fight, I have finished the race, I have kept the faith." (2 Timothy 4:7 NIV)

My passion for poetry helped shape (and continues to shape) this transition in my life, this turning point. Through words, God was giving me a deeper understanding of who I was and my place in this world.

At this point, there was an awaking happening within me. One of the hardest things a person can do is to look in the mirror. After you look at the reflection that is peering back at you, you can no longer deny what picture you have painted of yourself. You can no longer hide who you have become at that point.

PAIN WITH NO CHASER

I've got to get these words out of my head,
And when I put these words to paper,
It's like they wake up the dead
And breathe life into "this,"
So I can live this.

Even when I want to quit,
I have these words and that's it:
Just these words inside,
Just these words to make me feel alive
Because – without them –
I would have been committed suicide
And eradicated my flesh from this earth.
If it were up to the Devil,
I wouldn't be worth the air that I breathe.
I sometimes find it hard to believe
That God has a plan for me,
That this society has a plan for me,
Whether it be penitentiary or poverty.
The main thing that bothers me
Is that, for the majority of Blacks,
Getting out of being poor
Means having to play the lottery.
You think that because I'm from the suburbs
I am the exception.
All it takes is one paycheck
To put me in the same direction,

So I see these words as my reflections
Because someone besides me needs a resurrection.

This is not about being self-righteous;
This is about wanting to be free
And knowing what the price is.
Shoot!
I am 30+ years old and I'm still trying to find out
What the meaning of life is.
You don't have to be in prison
To know what hard time is.
We all are in a prison.
The only difference is what cell you're in.
That's why I hate Sundays,
Because, for me, it means back to Hell again.

My life has never been Hollywood
Because Hollywood is made for stars,
And the only stars I chased in my life
Were the ones in strip bars to strip these scars away.
"Dropping it like it's hot" isn't enough
To take the pain away.
Don't dare look at me that way.
You have insecurities, too.
The only difference between me and you
Is I refuse to tuck mine away,
Hoping that this last sip of "Henney"
Will erase away the stain on my brain.

These are the days when I feel I let my mother down,
But it's not about how long you're lost;
It's when you're finally found.
So, I keep my nose to the ground
And my eyes to the skies.
I only believe 10% of what I hear
Because 90% is nothing but lies,
And mama didn't raise any fool
But I acted too much a fool
When I spent more time slinging the tool
Then focusing on school.

Want to make a slave?
Hide the key in a book.
Want to go platinum?
Just write some bubble-gum lyrics and a catchy hook,
Because there are plenty of cities
Full of half-time crooks
Too scared to look in the mirror.
I'm taking the frost from the mirror of my life
And hoping I can see my days a little clearer.

A BETTER MAN

If God made the world,
Then I can make a better man.
It's not rocket science; it's magic.
Amel Larrieux said to "reach out and grab it,"
So I tried to keep praying,
But I couldn't pray enough,
And I tried to know the science,
But I couldn't add it up,
So I grabbed my ink and my pad
And got tatted up.
I felt better, man,
Because God knows I'm trying to be a better man,
Because the man from yesterday
Seems better than the man from today.
There are a lot of young black men
Who can't seem to find a way,
And it is going to take more
Than getting own our knees to pray.
Like the song says,

"Someday we will all be free"

But sometimes I ask myself if that "someday"
Is really meant for me.
That voice inside of me says

"Someday you will see"

So until then,
Call me Colin Ferguson with a purpose.
I'm trying to kill that part of me that is worthless
Because God knows I need to get my life in order.
I heard Lauryn Hill say

"It's just like water"

So I just want to get a taste.
Let my cup runneth over with His grace
Because there is no place like a peace of mind,
And the more I try to get there,
The more they try to take what is mine.
I wasn't born with a silver spoon.
I'm a black man in America.
That means I've got to take what is mine –
Or, shall I say, theirs,
Because it's not my life?
My life was sacrificed to the ancestors a long time ago.
It's theirs.
I want these words to sing for me like Roy Ayers
Because coffee has always been this man's color.
I want to be a better man like my older brother
Who finally found his lover and made her his wife.
Sometimes, I feel like Jay-Z.

"This can't be life"

I'm looking at the man in the mirror saying,

"This can't be right!"

So, I went back to school to get more light
And got a 4.0 my first semester.
Man, I'm high as a kite
And the herb hasn't even come around.
In order to be a better man,
I must turn *my* life around
Because no one is going to do it for me
Because most of this world chooses to ignore me
And life is like a horror flick:
A little too gory.
But, in this story, this black man survives.

We need to be better men –
Not just for ourselves,
But for our children and our wives
So that we can finally improve the quality of our lives.

We can be like guides to the future
And suture the wounds of the past,
Surpassing all tough breaks and mistakes
To make the statement
That, man, I am alive and I have no fear,
And to let these women know
That their better man
Is here.

ESTRANGED

Papa was a rolling stone.
He would roll his stones into a few homes
And leave behind disenfranchised lives
From the United States to South Korea.
He fought in the Korean War
(Just another war that didn't make sense).
He didn't have enough time or cents
To qualify for Father of the Year –
Just years and years of hate amongst mothers,
Of half brothers and half sisters not
Knowing each other,
And him not even knowing if one child
Bore his last name.
I can barely remember when he last came –
Not even to see me take my bride.
I cried many times as a child,
But my pen runs wild in pain
Trying to hold on to good moments in vain,
And God forgives.
I'm finally coming to grips with having to live
Barely knowing a father
And him not really knowing me.
Too many empty promises were left
With a child next to unfulfilled luggage
And unfulfilled days.
In many ways, my mind was filled with neglect,
And he wonders why I don't call much.

It's because my feelings can't connect
Or let the sins of my father's past
Be my sins today or any day.
I am no Anubis, so I can't weigh
His heart on a scale,
But, where he failed,
I must succeed.
To live a life just to breed
And not work hard to feed your kids
Is no life to lead.
Not being there to see your child grow
Is not sowing good seed.
I could never hate you,
Just like I can't make you work on making things right.
That's not my fight.
I just have to bite my pride.
Jesus died for me
So I don't have to die inside.
I have to do more on this Earth than just buy my time.
I must ride out the typhoon
And stay steadfast like a pontoon,
For even monsoons have to cease.
This is not a diss poem;
This is my release.

THOUGHTS OF THE PAST

Poetry found me at a time when I didn't know its many forms. Free verse, sonnets, and haiku weren't in my mental encyclopedia. When was the last time you saw one of those? It wasn't until I was introduced to Jeffrey Carroll, senior advisor to the Bergen County NAACP Youth Council at the time, that I would be charged to write a poem for the organization's Kwanzaa celebration. Jeff noticed that I wrote rhymes, and I guess he wanted me to apply my talent to another form of The Art. This was the first time I ever wrote anything with the intent of it being a poem. This meant the world to me, for I wasn't writing for a class project. This was to celebrate the beauty and struggle of a people in a society that still fights to deal with its own sickness, as well as the sickness of others. Racism is real no matter how this society likes to pretend that it doesn't exist. The poem I was to write made me step away from my individual pain and explore the pain of an entire race.

Thus, the poem Soul Survivor was born. This poem takes a trip back in time, and looks into the eyes of my ancestors who had their first encounters with another race. Gleaning knowledge from the many books I read about the African Holocaust, I was able to paint a picture of what the experience was like for my African ancestors who encountered the first slave traders. The Africans who survived the ordeal could only do so by virtue of their inextinguishable spirits. This poem was to remind myself, first and foremost, that I must persevere throughout my trials and tribulations with this same spirit.

"Those who cannot remember the past are condemned to repeat it." – George Santayana

SOUL SURVIVOR

The day heralds an ominous misfortune.
Dark clouds swallow the sun.
What evil lurks beyond the hills?
Who among us brings the mist of Hell?

A thousand pale-faced men suddenly exist.
Are these men from the Creator or the army from Hell?
Why do they come to our land,
Beautiful Africa?

Horror! Horror! Horror!

Pale-faced men attack us:
They plunder our village.
Homes are set on fire.
My eyes record the agonizing expressions
On my family's faces,
Malicious beatings,
a dark red bloodbath.

Horror! Horror! Horror!

No!
Not my friend!
No!
Not my father!
No!

My wife is dragged away in shackles.
Oh, Creator, what is next?

Tears form rivers down my face.
Our homes turn to smoke.
Pale-faced men are coming towards me.

No! No! No!

A violent blow strikes my head.
My body topples to the ground,
Stagnant,
Unconsciousness
Surrounded by darkness.

Portals of light break the eclipse.
My body is numbed by the restraints.
I am engulfed by men and women I do not know.
I've not a single shred of knowledge of the inevitable.
I'm lost in language,
Lost in despair,
But not lost in the soul.

THOUGHTS OF THE FUTURE

One of my favorite Billie Holiday songs is "God Bless the Child." This song was one of those socially conscious songs that made people fall in love with Lady Day, one of the most prominent jazz singers of her time. In this song, she seems to baptize the hopes and dreams of a better future for our children in the promise of God's love. Listening to this song, I would always envision hardworking African-American parents throughout inner cities working hard and struggling to create a different legacy for their children. These are the same parents who are never shaken by the poverty or pestilence around them. I can almost remote-view an event in their life, seeing them smiling inwardly and outwardly at the thought that, with God, their children would be alright. They would be alright, and Billie Holiday made them believe it. Despite what society might think, I still believe that today.

Working as a math tutor for inner-city kids in the summer of my freshman year of college changed my life. Seeing those kids with so much hope in their eyes, despite a state-controlled school system, kept me awake on plenty of nights in my dorm room, playing back those teenagers' words. They would tell me how their teachers would give them busy work and teach them rudimentary math skills. It broke my heart. Not all inner-city teachers are like this, but the ones who are indirectly affect future prison populations. Some of you may think that is harsh, but there are only two choices for these kids: Do well in school to break the cycle, or be a part of the prison-industrial complex. God bless the teachers who care.

I remember one kid specifically because he never possessed a calculator in his life. You should have seen his face when I gave him my brand-new Texas Instruments scientific calculator that I brought from the school bookstore. If you were an engineering student, you know those calculators weren't cheap, but the value of how good that adolescent felt was priceless. I had to succeed for these kids. Thus, I poured into them all of the math tricks and knowledge I knew in order to improve and enhance their math skills. The calculator I gave to that kid, by the way, was a reward for the good grades he got in math. I don't know where he is now, or if he went on to college, or what. But a part of me feels that he is alright.

This next poem is for the child who doesn't have his or her own. If you are fortunate enough to read this book, pass on these words to a teenager like this. If you are this child right now, I pray that you find someone who stands out to you as a person of good moral character, and who represents all of the things that you are not, but want to be, despite not knowing how. Seek their guidance. Study their habits. Realize that there is a world that you can – and will – master. Dream of better days, and with each small step towards them, live better days. You are not alone. God is with you.

A CHILD WHO DOESN'T HAVE ITS OWN

"Mama may have,
Papa may have,
But God bless the child
That's got its own."

– Billie Holiday

But what if a child doesn't have its own?
If he never had his own,
If he was grown in a world where
Home is every street corner
And every block
Where shots are heard in the distance like clockwork?
What if a child can't work
Because he or she is not old enough,
But they can work for the streets
Because he or she only
Has to be bold enough
Or somewhat tough?

What if a child attends a school that doesn't care,
Where teachers are too scared to teach them the tools
they need to succeed in a society that believes
That, if you're black,
Then you're cursed,
And, if you're poor,
Your life is not worth one cent?

What if a child has a mother
Who can barely pay the rent
Because she's always cracked out
And has a daddy who backed out of being a father?

What if a child doesn't bother to think
About the people, he or she steals from,
Or if he or she killed someone
In the process?

What if a girl grows up thinking
That love is nothing but sex,
And that, if she doesn't give it up,
Then she will be his ex?

What if a child feels there is nothing left to do,
No paradise to look forward to
And that the option left
Is take his or her own life
And their soul to rest?
Will this same child still be blessed?

GOD-MIND

I am the voice that is always heard,
Guided by the spirit,
Blessing every word,
Giving birth to the lifeless
And bringing death to the soulless.
Where I rest, no man or woman can ever see.
I am the thought transcending your mentality.
Take a deep breath.
Feel that energy?
I am mathematics and science
Put into action,
And a divine revelation is your reaction.
Like an infinite fraction,
I am indivisible,
And my physical form is invisible:
God-mind in the mind.

'TILL NEXT WE MEET AT THE LAUNDROMAT

I walk into the Laundromat with another load,
Another ordeal,
Entangled in confusion as my eyes stay fixed
On the ever-turning wheels.
I'm lost in bold colors –
Black,
Brown,
Red,
Yellow –
I receive a quarter
(a thousand thanks to that beneficent fellow).
I insert the coins that launch the colors' fate,
Drowning and spinning,
Controlled like their fellow mates,
Powerless to the perpetual conditions that exist –
Colorful clothes, but hidden
By the abundant bubbles of Wisk,
Drowning again and again.
When will this madness cease,
Confined and contained like a criminal
In the belly of the beast?
The spinning returns
Then, an abrupt
Time gap follows
(Another day, another load)
'Til next we meet at the laundromat.

BLUE

What if I woke up one morning in a blue world,
And even I was blue?
What if I lived on a blue block
With blue neighbors,
And we all sang the blues –
Not because we were sad,
But because the song reminded us of a time
When we were once a different shade
Though, now, we are all one shade:
Blue?

Not baby blue
Or cyan blue –
Just royal blue?
There would be no fighting between
Darker blues and lighter blues
Because the darker blues
Think the lighter blues are not true blues –
Just one hue:
Blue.

What if I woke up in a blue nation
That was truly

"One nation, under God"

And no fighting amongst other nations

Or other people
Because they praise the same God –
Yes,
The same God,
But in different ways.
There would be blue bliss,
For the world would have blue unity
On a blue planet.

I could walk in Bloomingdales with a blue bag
Wearing blue jeans and a blue hoodie
Without people thinking
I was going to steal from the place,
Or I could walk into
Big Blue's office (also known as IBM)
With a resume in one hand
And the ambition to become CEO
One day, for there, would be
No such thing as a glass ceiling,
And I would buy a JetBlue airplane
And fly across America
Because I would be free.
Yes,
I would be free.
Yes,
I would be blue and free,
But I wouldn't stop there.

I would write blue poetry
And put it in a blue book with black print
And talk about blue people
And how beautiful it is to be blue,
To be blue and proud,
Because we would all be free.
Yes,
We would *all* be free.

"I want my people to be free
To be free
All my people to be free to be free"

To be
Free.

DEFINE YOU

You have filled the spaces in my life like spackling
You sweeten my soul like saccharin
And taught silence how to speak.
You made beats out of my heartbeat.
Your voice hits waves
Beyond measurable octaves
And make my straight lines concave,
Causing rocks to dissolve
And problems to be solved.

You make my blues green
And make my life more than what it seemed:
A dream preserved,
Not a dream deferred.
You are truly what I deserve.
You are that state in which matter turns to energy,
Where mathematics becomes symmetry
And where thoughts become poetry.

You are the after-effect,
The result of a catalyst
When sex becomes orgasmic,
Beats become rhythm,
And thoughts become reasons.
You are the image after the translation from the brain,
Meaning without words:
The flow after the drop, the flux,

The diamond after the rough.
You can't be cloned.
You own this world.
You are the woman after the girl
Who would make a bum dress to the nines.
You can't be confined
Or defined.
You were made to be adored.
You are in the distance like the moon
To, one day, be explored.

MY GODDESS

I always wondered what an angel
Looked like when nights
Seemed to stretch
To the end of the universe.

Then, you appeared
Through a ray of light:
A black, angelic, divine,
Sweet, diamond-eyed face.
Just the mere thought
Of the taste of your Nubian lips
Could bring this brother peace
Like the Bloods and the Crips.
You make the silence speak
As I become weak
From your smile
And your grace.
I'm probing every inch and space
Of your perimeters with my eyes
And matching the area and size of your mind
Combined with your spirituality.

It's kind of like a dreamer's dream
When love is out of reach.
Like a Caribbean beach,
I want to take refuge in you
And be by your side like a tattoo.

With every stride, you take
Me on a ride across the Atlantic.
A gigantic of a woman you are.
Your mind spans the stretch of time,
Lands on earth and touches the stars.

You are a picture painted perfectly,
With every stroke. Your paralyzing stares invoke me,
And provoke me to capture you in my arms
And to take up arms against your enemies.
With love divine,
Baptized in your shrine,
I am blessed
To be in the company
Of such an empress.

Let me stress the fact
That I am at your mercy,
And that my life is thirsty for your love.
Filled with truth,
You are the living proof
That love is beautiful
And that love is worth feeling.

THE ONE

It's not that she doesn't care.
It's more like she cares too much,
But it seems that she has the whole earth
On her shoulders,
The whole young, black population on her shoulders.
I saw her spirit dance with the ancestors
Of past philanthropists,
    Abolitionists,
    Spiritualists,
    Educators
    And soul-motivators.

I saw her give hope to hopeless children
Who were trying to survive streets without a heartbeat
And as cold as concrete,
Where crackheads were like the walking dead,
Thursday nights are gang-initiation nights,
And these children have no choice but to fight.
She is the light through their tunnel vision eyes.

No ocean of adversities
Or a mountain of doubt blocks her path.
Her purpose was written in the stars
And solidified by her actions.
Thus, she is God's gift to our race,
And, though she may face trial after trial,
And struggle after struggle,

I know she will survive.
She keeps my hope alive,
For I bear witness to her greatness, which is love.
When I am in her presence,
All I feel is love.

She is like a modern–day Harriet Tubman,
Bringing our children to the Promised Land.
She may deny her strength,
But I won't.
She may forget our past,
But I don't, for it is etched in my mind.
I find comfort in her,
For, in this black hole of a world,
She's my new horizon at the end of an event horizon.
She's my heaven after a walk through Hell.

As she walks, she sings
Dizzy Gillespie's "A Night in Tunisia" with every step,
And, when she probes into my eyes,
She telepathically opens my mind to her divine.
I will walk over a thousand landmines to protect her.
She could let her tears saturate me so,
Like Sade, she would

"Feel No Pain."

She could lose the whole world,
But would have me to gain

I see countless people
Thrive off of her energy.
She brings symmetry to my world of chaos,
So it's no wonder why I love her,
And it's because of that love
That I would go to the chair for her.

This love burns eternal.
She sends an inferno through me
As she soothes me with her seductive tone.
Every chromosome in my body
Believes she is the one for me.
You see, before her,
I thought I found love,
But it wasn't until her that love found me.

She is the teacher
And the lover intertwined.
She is the thought and the desire in my mind —
My Betty Shabazz,
My Assata Shakur,
And my Alice Walker,
All in one.
Every day, I am striving to be her Malcolm X,
Her Langston Hughes,
And her David Walker
(Just to name some).

Let us have no endings –
Only new beginnings.
Whether in friendship or in love,
In my heart and in my mind,
We will always be inseparable.

FREE ME

My soul has been captive for so long.
"Unchain My Heart" like Ray Charles
And join me in a sing–along to an old Negro spiritual.
I need that miracle only a saint as you can give
So that I may live again, be reborn.
You baptized me in your gospel.
I am your disciple.
So, what is your sermon?
Chase these vermin from my temple.
Purify my mental.
Send your love from the outskirts
And make it residential.

Free me.
Give me my freedom papers.
If not,
Then pick me up on your underground railroad
So I can escape to your love like Canada.
I can't stand the thought
Of wearing these chains another day.
I know you know the way.
I know you know what to say.
Or, let me be that runaway slave.
Let me be your Cinque and you can "Give Us Free."
We can be as strong as El-Hajj Malik El-Shabazz
And Betty Shabazz and overcome this Wizard of Oz
They call America.

Free me
So that I can always celebrate my day of my Jubilee.
We can help rebuild Black Wall Street
Into something more concrete:
A strong foundation to save ourselves
And, then, this nation.
Make today feel like1865.
Make me feel alive again.
With you, I will always win.
Come, release me.
Come, unleash me
So my freedom can begin.
Free me.

THE GREAT O' US OF A II. (MORE POLY-TRICKS)

How many times are we going to be lied to
When we realize that the American dream
Is nothing but streams of polluted drinking water
With artificial preservatives
Bottled up in fancy packages
And sold on every newsstand for 50 cents,
Polluting more minds?

How we were so quick to raise that banner
When the government spreads more propaganda
Taking sides between Palestinians and Israel?
And you wonder why Al Qaeda got real on us
When they devoured the Twin Towers
Turning innocent lives to flames
With commuter planes.
It makes me wonder who was eviler:
Bush or Bin Laden?
While the American public still waited for Bush
To give us an answer
As to why he gave the order to spread
Through Iraq like cancer though not one weapon
Of mass destruction was found.

I tell you:
It is the same poly-tricks
That can cause a President to be elected
Off of fixed ballots giving new meaning to

"The ballot or the bullet"

And more and more cops like to pull it on black lives.
I try to make sense of it,
But my soul won't allow me to justify it.

It amazes me how Congress can vote to get a raise,
But you have to fight just to make sure
You get paid what you're supposed to be paid,
And the US spends more money on sending aid
When there are still more homeless
And jobless people to save.

This country's got it backward.
It seems like actors make better politicians,
But this is the Great 'O U.S. of A,
Where we fund the greatest terrorists the world
Have ever seen,
Where companies like Enron
Take our hard-earned green
And CEOs got money busting at the seams.

But, don't call me liberal or leftist,
Or put me on the FBI list.
I want to be like Lenny Kravitz,
Trying to find a reason for America
To live another season.
Are we

"Bowling for Columbine" like Michael Moore,
Or are we spending more time
Trying to castrate Michael Jackson
For his weird actions,
Like how we watched the outcome
Of the Kobe Bryant issue
And misusing the media to promote
The Bigga Thomas mentality?

What a society we live in.
What country we live in,
When priest gets away with touching the children.
I'm not anti–U.S.
I'm just tired of the mess
That this country makes and has made
While the good American people
Are the ones to get played every day.
But, you should expect nothing less,
From The Great 'O U.S. Of A.

THE EVIL THAT MEN DO

She was 16 years old
When her innocence was spoiled,
Soiled by a so-called boyfriend,
Who pretended he was a friend.
He locked her in a room
To seal her inevitable doom,
So much so that not even a man in a red cape
Could save her.
He made her do things against her will.
Though she's still alive,
Her spirit was killed.

Now, she is a victim of his lust.
There's no man she can trust,
So she lives her life too promiscuously.
She's trying to control now
What she couldn't control then,
But she shouldn't have to be the blame
For another person's sin.
I send a prayer to Heaven to see her through.
I hope she realizes that it's not her fault,
It's the evil that men do to her.

His name was synonymous with God,
But, in reality, his actions defined the Devil,
And, on several occasions, he made her taste Hell.
A prisoner of fear, her bedroom was her jail cell.

Thus, her sentence was to serve a four-year sentence
Of relentless beatings
And four years of lying and cheating.
God knows her life was rough.
Then, one day, God gave her the strength of J-Lo
To say she'd had enough.

The place where she rested her head
Is no longer her deathbed.
No more treating her life like fight night
With a purse two times less than her worth,
Because, in her life, he has no more time invested.
The only time he had was the time before
He got arrested,
And, now, there is no more hell to come home to.
She is no longer a victim of the evil that men do.

MONEY MATTERS

I couldn't afford the Galaxy S5,
So I settled for the Galaxy S4.
Why is it that, even when the money is less,
We still want more?
I guess that is the difference
Between the rich and the poor.
One is like a moth to the flame,
And the other makes flame live more.

Capitalism has been on a world tour.
Control the world resources
And you create a world war.
You're expecting the government to bail you out
When the national debt is about
$18 trillion and counting.
I am seriously doubting that they can save themselves.
You better stop pouting
And save yourselves
Because nothing is given for free.
You may not pay now,
But you better believe he is coming for his fee.

Politics:
Where the rich play us like a ball and a stick.
We don't want to stand on a voting line,
But wait for hours on line for a pair of kicks.
The game is fixed,

In case you didn't know;
You surely know now.
If you want to win in life,
Here are a few ways how:

Get free,
Get out of debt,
And take care of your family.
Save your chips
And get wealthy,
And then give to the poor.
Help your fellow man and woman
And pray a little more
Because, in God's eyes, you will always be a star.
See, I remember days when I used to waste
My dollars in strip bars.
Now, I place my dollars in mason jars,

Trying to make a mountain out of a molehill
And praying that all this hard work doesn't kill.
It is better to chase a dream than to chase a dollar bill,
For we all are all like Lauryn:
Trying to make it to the top of the hill.
God gave you a beautiful gift called "free will,"
Meaning that you can will the worse parts of you
Into the best parts of you.
You have to start walking
For God to do something great for you.
Let your dreams be a monument of you.

The Good Book says

"The borrower is slave to the lender,"

So I borrow less
To be less of a slave.
Dave Ramsey says,

"We got to make our money behave."

No matter what people profess,
You're nowhere near worthless.
Delete your fears and be guided to your success,
Lest you make a mess of things yourself.
Make money;
Don't let the money make yourself.

MR. POOR

You know me, and your parents know me,
But you are trying to walk around like
You've outgrown me,
Like you can out–income me.
Look at your bank statement.
You don't have a pot in which pee.
You let people in the same position you are
Try to tell you how to be.
You're so silly.

I mastered the math.
All I have to do is take away your dreams
To dictate your path,
To tell you that you don't have a craft
Or know how to make people laugh,
That you can't rap or sing
And will never make the NBA draft.

You should be happy with what you have.
But, like that little girl in the AT&T commercial,

"We want more; we want more!"

You've got to have that house you can't afford.
You've got to have a credit score,
But wealthy people pay with cash.
They never see me: Mr. Poor.

You still don't know who I am.

I'm that four percent inflation rate that's keeping
You from getting ahead.
I'm that Medicare Budget cut
Preventing you from getting your meds,
Meaning you're dead in the water in two ways:
All it takes for you to be poor is two pays
Because you never saved for those rainy days.
Even if you win the lottery, you'll be broke tomorrow
Because you haven't changed your ways
And you rather have stuff now than be content today.

Pay for things with that plastic.
I'll make you believe you need one
Just in case things get dramatic.
Now, you are in serious debt
And living in your parent's attic.
You're a brand-name fanatic.
You're a shop-at-the-mall-every-payday addict
Who thinks that all your problems will be solved
If you always vote Democratic,
But the Republicans are the same joke
Hidden beneath different smoke.
The law of supply and demand
Has got you all in the same boat,
Like the one, your ancestors came in.
Then, you promote me to everyone you know
Without me even lifting a pen.

You've never heard of living below your means.
You've never heard of living on rice and beans.
You've got to have the latest trend
And got to wear this season's jeans.

The funny thing is
That I'm your enemy
And you don't even know it.
God can give you a one-dollar blessing,
But you would bury it in the ground
Instead of growing it.
They call me Mr. Poor.

HAVE YOU EVER

Have you ever taken your last breath
When there's nothing left to give or take,
When the only thing you can do
Is to suffocate and fall on deaf ears
That only hear the aftermath of wrath
That lasted a thousand years?
When you shed your thousandth tear
And the rest is dried upon your face?
When the truth can no longer be erased
From your mind and you can only dwell
In an everlasting Hell in which your name
Does not exist?

Have you ever felt that pain inside
When you've been running from your problems,
But there is nowhere you can hide?
When your baby daddy doesn't want to be a father
And you don't know what to do
Because your bills are piled to the ceiling,
And all you need is a blessing to get you through?

When you've been laid-off from your job
And there's no more bread for the honey,
And you're about to get evicted
Because you haven't paid that money?
There's nothing funny about this picture.
Your pockets seem to get poorer and poorer,

While theirs keep getting richer and richer.
You borrow money you can't payback for weeks,
And the more you seem to get ahead,
The harder it becomes to get on your feet.

Have you ever felt like you were on the other side
Of a barrel with your eyes on the violence of death
Though His eye is on the sparrow?
When you're trying to look for God
But you can't see the god in you,
And heaven keeps knocking at your door
But you won't let it walk on through?

You have got to believe in these words:
If you don't believe in yourself –
Because what I see before me
Is worth more than fame and wealth –
You have to take that gun off of the top shelf
And kill that part of you that is hazardous
To your health.

You've got to lay all your burdens
Down by the riverside,
And, then,
And only then,
Will you see the Most High.

Have you ever wanted a miracle?
Well, that day is here, and the answer?
You can't get it from your man.
You can get it from a paycheck
Or from someone else's hands.
It's spiritual.

SPEAK LIFE

I was tired of being uninspired,
So I woke myself up
And I told myself to look into the light
So that I could know what it was like to have a dream
And pursue it,
To cascade over obstacles like fluid
And make people wonder where that power came from,
To overcome fear by speaking life
Until, suddenly, a door opened.
I was coping with so-called friends holding me back.
I want to strap on "...the whole armor of God"
And pound the earth like a steel rod,
Creating a natural landmark
To benchmark my accomplishments
And give souls something else to follow.
I want to fill that emptiness that was once hollow
Like a throat that can swallow again,
Like a pen that can write again
Until not just I,
But all of us can win
By not just saving one,
But saving more.
We are the explorers of life's great outdoors.
We're not quite perfect
But recreated over
Until God makes us perfect
And over-made,

Until every day is like a parade
To unmask the charade
And walk into our own realities,
So that, just like this poem, we transform our "me"
Until the "me" no longer exists,
Until this Hell of a world no longer exists,
And, one day, we live in eternal bliss.

THOUGHTS OF FOREVER

Proposing to my now wife was the scariest thing I've ever had to do. It wasn't because I doubted that I was making the right decision. I just didn't want to mess up this momentous night. I wrote a poem and chose not to remember the poem, in fear that I would mess it up in the process of trying to propose. Also, I had no clue whether was going to say "yes." Too often, you will see those proposals on TV, where the girlfriend says, "I'll think about it." My heart would drop in my chest if that happened to me. Thank God it didn't.

Up until this point, I almost completely gave up on trying to pursue a serious relationship. A lot of it, of course, was my fault, due to my consistently bad decision–making that lasted well into my 30s. In order to break this cycle, I had to change. My definition of manhood had to be revisited. This journey to find who God wanted me to be would ultimately prepare me for the woman of my life. Once I met and got to know Angela, it was pretty much only a matter of time before I knew I would make that commitment.

The next poem is the proposal poem that I wrote for her. Each word completely expresses how I felt then, and how I still feel to this day. Society teaches us that you get married when you find that perfect someone for you. The reality is that you become the perfect person for each other as you build your relationship. Both of you bring something special to the relationship that makes your union whole. I thank God for her, and for making us whole.

MY FOREVER

This poem is for you,
And there is nothing anonymous about us.
Angela, you exist in the physical,
But your name is short for "angel,"
Meaning that God has used you to bring the Devil out
of me.
Spiritually, you were made in Heaven for me.
God planned you before me,
But we have so much in common
That most people would think you were a clone of me.
Your spirit has grown in me like a fruit of the vine.
We combined like Voltron to defend His throne.
Our souls come together like two-toned jeans.
We are brought together by the seams.

You add that island flavor to my crock pot.
Just lick my fingers and slop up that last bit.
Our love doesn't quit.
It's stronger than the George Washington Bridge
supports.
We are two continents, but
Our ports have an equal amount of traffic
Going to and fro.
We go beyond the grain.
Our love can't be contained;
It spreads like a wildfire.
It spreads like data through the wire,

And I aspire to be the best man God allows me to be.
We are like symmetry on a canvas.
It amazes me how God planned this.
It all started with a chance meeting –
Stimulating conversations and warm greetings,
An email shot in the dark,
An unforgettable night under the stars talking in a
park,

And lunch and dinner dates
'Til they turned into sharing future plans
To create something more animated than the
Animatrix.
I've got no magic tricks up my sleeve,
But the God in me can accomplish anything
As long as I believe.
With Him, there's no negative action that we can't
supersede.
He gives us permanent power over evil,
Not just a reprieve.
We can be like Ossie Davis and Ruby Dee.

Just call me your Wall–E.
You are my Eve –
Not the one who ate the forbidden fruit.
You are *my* Eve, the one with Jamaican roots
And values passed down like stewed peas
And callaloo.
When I need to talk to someone,

I know I can call on you
To give me a scripture
That'll get me through
And to make me feel that I can do more than make do,
That my life is worth more than the money owed
To finish that Xanadu project.
Until I met you,
I was searching for love with no prospects.
You project your love at the right angle
Like a dart to the heart.
You turn love into an art form.
I truly believe that we were born together.
The only thing left to say is,

"Will you be my forever?"

CONCLUSION

You have completed the journey from *Lost in Space* to *Sucked in and Torn Apart,* and *Beyond the Event Horizon (Paradigm Shift).* You've witnessed the power of a black hole. It destroyed me, rebuilt me, and, ultimately, brought me closer to my true self. The journey through is always the toughest, but the rewards are mind-blowing. This new universe is so rich with purpose. Fear can cloud your purpose.

There's a quote from the movie "Dune" that I will never forget: "Fear is the mind killer." That couldn't be any truer. Fear was getting in the way of my passion. My passion has always been poetry. It has brought me *Beyond the Event Horizon.* My spirit has been renewed. My direction has been made clear. I pray that you accept your passion if you haven't already. I pray that you've reconnected with your passion to find your true position in life. If opening myself up to you through my poetry has helped you see what's already within you, then I have done my job. You followed me this far. Your next journey is your story. Live it!

ABOUT THE AUTHOR

James C. Ellerbe was born and currently lives, in New Jersey with his wife. He graduated from Hackensack High School and Gibbs College (formerly in Livingston, New Jersey) with an Associate's Degree in Computer Network Administration.

He has appeared on a BET's "Buy the Book" and a non-taped edition of the world-renowned "Showtime at the Apollo" showcase in which he and other poets helped promote the first spoken-word event at a venue called "Poetic Battles." He represented New Jersey's team for this event. He also performed at the Kola Note (Site of Montreal, Canada's Jazz festival), Elizabeth High School, Rutgers University, NJIT, Fairleigh Dickinson University, and Sarah Lawrence College, and appeared on WLIB Radio NYC.

Recently, James was also a finalist for the 2017 Indie Author Legacy Award for Poet of the Year and featured author at the BCCLS BooksNJ 2015 and 2017 Book Festivals at Paramus Library in Paramus, NJ. He also wrote and co-produced his three-act play, "A Dream Preserved." "Beyond the Event Horizon" is his first book of poetry released in April 2015, and "Pulsar" is his first spoken word album released by Not Enough Words LLC on April 2018.

Contact us for more books.
Not Enough Words LLC
(973) 910-1865
newllcinfo@gmail.com
www.JamesCEllerbe.com

36578422R00097

Made in the USA
Middletown, DE
16 February 2019